CRYSTAL REIKI

CRYSTAL REIKI

A Handbook for Healing Mind, Body, and Soul

KRISTA MITCHELL

author of *Change Your Energy*

STERLING ETHOS
New York

STERLING EPICURE
New York

An Imprint of Sterling Publishing Co., Inc.
1166 Avenue of the Americas
New York, NY 10036

ISBN 978-1-4549-3025-9

Distributed in Canada by Sterling Publishing Co., Inc.
c/o Canadian Manda Group, 664 Annette Street
Toronto, Ontario M6S 2C8, Canada
Distributed in the United Kingdom by GMC Distribution Services
Castle Place, 166 High Street, Lewes, East Sussex BN7 1XU, England
Distributed in Australia by NewSouth Books
University of New South Wales, Sydney, NSW 2052, Australia

For information about custom editions, special sales, and
premium and corporate purchases, please contact Sterling Special Sales
at 800-805-5489 or specialsales@sterlingpublishing.com.

Manufactured in China

2 4 6 8 10 9 7 5 3

sterlingpublishing.com

Cover Design by Igor Satanovsky
Interior Design by Sharon Murray Jacobs
Image Credits: Caroline M. Casey (stone illustrations):
iii, 16, 23, 56, 59, 60, 91, 93, 105, 113, 121, 124, 125, 128, 129, 131, 135,
142, 143, 146–147, 158, 154, 166, 188, 189, 190, 191, 211;
All other images from iStock and Shutterstock

CONTENTS

INTRODUCTION

Being a healer is a noble calling.

As I typed these words, I'm looking out my writing room window to the great maple tree in my back garden, to the busy country road with people driving home from work. I'm surrounded by my crystals, metaphysical books, and candles that have been charmed with reiki and sacred oils. My dogs are sleeping at my feet. My altar to my ancestors is on my right, and photographic prints of New York City, taken by an artist friend, hang on the wall to my left. And I'm thinking: "I've come a long way." It feels like it was a lifetime ago that I, rather timidly, built a small e-mailing list of friends' names and addresses, and hit SEND on the message announcing that I was offering my first professional reiki sessions.

It's been almost fifteen years since then, and I'm now a published author on crystal healing. I've performed thousands of professional Crystal Reiki sessions, taught numerous certification courses, conducted countless workshops, given talks, and led guided crystal meditations and rituals both online and all over North America. I've gone from being dismissed when I say I am a crystal healer, to being interviewed for print and online magazines like *Vanity Fair*, the *Huffington Post*, *Today*, *Elle*, and *New York* magazine. It's been a pretty wild ride so far, fueled by my passion for crystals, healing, and spirituality, and it's been a lot of hard work, but that hard work continues to pay off.

My purpose in writing this book is to teach you the art of Crystal Reiki, a combination of two healing modalities and a system of healing that I developed during my years of professional energy work in New York City. But it's also my story as a healer and what I learned from being a professional energy worker—from offering alternative therapy to a wide cross section of big city people, to developing the guts, magic, discipline, and faith it took to succeed as a spiritual healer.

I officially started my training and opened my practice in New York City in 2005. It was a trial by fire. Those were different times then, when people didn't believe you could earn a living from energy work, so most sought training for the sole benefit of their own spiritual growth and experience. I was the only student in my reiki class who, when asked, put my hand up and said I wanted to be a professional healer. It was a signal to the Universe.

A mere month after I'd earned my first degree in reiki, the first level of certification in the reiki system of natural healing, my teacher began referring clients to me because he was too busy with his day job to take them on. I remember feeling terrified on the subway ride to my first-ever client. Who was I to be doing this? What was I doing? I thought to myself, I DON'T KNOW WHAT I'M DOING!!!! But then a soothing message from my higher self cut in: "You're nervous because you care, and that's a good sign. Keep going." So I did.

I honestly didn't know at the time if reiki worked. I knew that I liked doing it, and people liked receiving it. I didn't believe that I could make it as a healer, and yet there seemed no other option. I felt compelled to pursue it. And so I did.

When I introduced crystals into my healing work, it was a game-changer. Rather than sitting quietly and listening to the hum of reiki as it flowed through me, I was now tuning in to the frequencies of my clients' chakras, gazing at their auras, hearing guidance from their spirit guides, and seeing visions of crystal placements and combinations that could help them. I was able to address people's needs more specifically, help accelerate their healing process, and work at a deeper and more engaged level than I had before. It felt like the possibilities and opportunities for my work were dramatically expanding, and that I'd found my true calling.

Despite the opening up of these new possibilities, it wasn't all rainbows and unicorns. In New York City, crazy high rent is a very real thing. And for someone who is an empath (someone who can feel energy and be influenced by other people's emotions), who was recovering from being broke and heartbroken, it was a hard place to live and a very challenging time. When the global investment banking company Lehman Brothers declared bankruptcy in 2008 and the United States hit an economic downturn, it was a scary time for everyone and probably the wrong time to be running a spiritual healing business. Or was it?

As I sit here and reflect on how much I've learned, I realize that I don't just have teachings to share about Crystal Reiki, but also wisdom to share on how to be a professional healer. I've had to peel myself off the floor many times. I've had failures and enormous fear. I've been wrong. I've called friends, bawling my eyes out and needing confirmation. I've had to grit my teeth and push past boundaries on every level to get to where I was headed. But I did it.

I've had dark nights of the soul when I wondered if I'd made the right choice. There were certainly jobs out there that could have been easier, more profitable, more securely established. But something about this work came from my soul, stirred my heart, and gave my life purpose and meaning. So I kept going, even when I despaired that I'd never make it.

Being a healer is a noble calling. It's deeply fulfilling work, and much needed in this world of ours. I read an article recently by Oprah Winfrey in which she said: "Everything you do that leaves a handprint or a heartprint is your legacy." I used to think that creating my system of Crystal Reiki healing was my legacy, that my first book, *Change Your Energy,* was my legacy, that the healers I trained in this work were my legacy. But I also helped people change their lives, heal, and transform, and, in the process, I, too, changed my life, healed, and transformed. It's *all* a part of my legacy.

To be a healer is to leave a handprint and a heartprint as your legacy. Your life is your school, your art is your work, your teachers are your clients, your modalities are your tools, and your path of mastery is lifelong. Always remember this, and in good times and bad, moments of triumph or failure, you will stay aligned with your calling and purpose.

I write this book about Crystal Reiki in service to you, dear healer, as you continue to pursue your calling and purpose. One of the things I've come to love about healers is that they are a tribe that is devoted to enriching their spiritual path and to advancing their healing knowledge. Thank you for being part of my tribe. The world needs you.

— *Krista Mitchell*

SOMEWHERE IN CANADA, 2017

HOW TO USE THIS BOOK

CRYSTAL REIKI is a holistic system of energy healing, and this book is based on the style of Crystal Reiki I developed while working full time for years as a professional spiritual healer in New York City. It's by no means meant to be a bible or to negate the value of other systems. What I can say about this one is that it was successful. It was tried and tested over years of in-person, professional client work, and everything I'm sharing has been culled from session notes, testimonials, case studies, anecdotes, and my own life experiences.

The purpose of this book is to teach reiki practitioners how to offer Crystal Reiki in a way that is safe, effective, and professional. It is therefore assumed that readers have already been trained in reiki, having at least received their first-degree certification. Many reiki practitioners worldwide intuitively add crystals or combine crystal healing with their reiki sessions. This book is meant to provide a solid foundation of knowledge and expertise that can support a reiki practitioner in offering Crystal Reiki as its own modality at a professional level of service.

You can use this book as a manual for your own education and training as a Crystal Reiki practitioner, as a reference book for crystal combinations and layouts to be used in your energy healing sessions, and to learn fundamental skills and expertise that are often required of a professional spiritual healer.

The book is structured to help guide you through the process of first learning about Crystal Reiki, including the background and history in Part 1: The Fundamentals; how to properly prepare for giving a Crystal Reiki session in Part 2: A Healer's Preparation; and then how to give a Crystal Reiki session, including crystal layouts and in-session techniques for physical, mental, emotional, spiritual, and aura healing in Part 3: The Practice.

Part 4: Self-Care for Healers provides guidelines and suggestions for crystal self-healing, self-care, and support for professional energy healers, again culled from years of my personal and professional experience. I consider Part 4 to be of particular importance, as healers tend to put their own care last, and yet have needs that are unique to their vocation. In some ways, Part 4 should really be at the start of the book, as healers' own health, well-being, and happiness are the foundation upon which everything else in their life and work rests.

My hope is that, in reading this book and using its information, you will deepen your healing skills and wisdom and be of greater service to your clients. Crystal blessings to you!

Part 1

THE FUNDAMENTALS

WHAT IS
CRYSTAL REIKI?

first started my career as a spiritual healer offering traditional

reiki sessions. Though I'd had a love of crystals and stones as

a child, and worked with them in my early adult life as talismans,

amulets, and to add potency to charms, I'd never considered using

them for physical, mental, or emotional healing. When a friend

of mine began studying crystal therapy, and suggested that we

swap energy sessions as a form of practice, I became aware of how

incredibly effective they could be. While I loved the overall warmth

and relaxation I felt from reiki, different crystals had a direct and

specific impact on how I was thinking and feeling.

I remember the first time I held a piece of tumbled selenite in my left hand, and after two minutes, I had transitioned into an altered state, almost as if I were feeling "high" or blissed out. I remember thinking, "Whoa!" and looking at the humble crystal in my hand. I could feel it clearing all the negative energy that was floating around and inside me. I was blown away that this small piece of selenite could have such a powerful effect on me, and it made me eager to learn about all kinds of crystals and how they could help me in my daily life and my healing practice. Every time I felt stressed or that my energy was too heavy, or if I needed to quickly relax and unwind before bed, I would hold that selenite crystal and begin to feel more serene, peaceful, light, and detached from my worries.

That first experience with selenite was enough to make me a passionate believer in the healing power of crystals. I was hooked, and began a yearlong practice of wearing or meditating with a different crystal every day, and making note of its effects on me.

One day it would be citrine, and I'd feel sunny and bright and more optimistic about my life. The next it would be pietersite, and while my intuition felt sharper, I'd also felt moody and anxious because it was bringing feelings to the surface that I'd been suppressing. Day after day I'd experience shifts in mood, temperament, the slow but steady healing of old emotional wounds, boosts in confidence and energy, strengthening of psychic abilities, the notes went on and on. I also experienced the downside of working with crystals—how they could imbalance you, bring more emotions to the surface than you were prepared to handle, make you feel ungrounded, spaced out, or out of your body at the wrong times, and more. The crystals were teaching me their myriad effects on the human body and energy system, as well as how to work with them responsibly and wisely, based on actual experience.

It occurred to me that if crystals could have this level of impact on me, they could also have a powerful impact on my reiki clients. I thus began combining the two systems, gradually adding more and more crystals to my reiki sessions, and taking notes on what worked, what didn't, any discoveries I was making, or new ways of working with their energy. I'd place select crystals on my clients' chakras, and then I'd go through my standard reiki hand placement protocols. The more I worked and received positive and encouraging feed-back from my clients, the more I fine-tuned the practice.

While both crystal therapy and reiki are beautiful modalities on their own, there was something special about combining the two: With the crystals I could address specific issues, either by clearing negative energy from the system (like pain, stress, or sadness), and/ or by providing the supportive energy a client needed (like calm, enhanced focus or vitality). With reiki I could help to bring overall balance to the system, deepen a client's sense of relaxation, and provide the nurturing energy my client needed to heal and transform. It was a total win-win, and it became my focus and specialty for over over a decade of professional healing work and personal development.

WHAT IS REIKI?

Reiki (pronounced RAY-kee) is a Japanese word that means "universal life-force energy." It is the energy force that flows around and through all living things, also known as chi or qi. In other cultures, this energy may be referred to as light, mana, prana, ether, ka, the unified field, or Jesod, to name just a few. This energy is older than history, quite likely predating life itself. It is believed that all life is formed from it. Reiki is also a form of energy healing that is intended to promote balance in all living systems. When you're channeling reiki, it enters your body from the crown and flows down through your heart center, down both arms, and out through your hands. It is channeled in accordance with divine intelligence and with the intention of providing healing energy for the highest healing good. It is subtle and cumulative in its effects, meaning that the more the reiki energy builds up in your system, the more it helps to restore balance. If you imagine an empty swimming pool with a shallow and deep end, reiki flows into a person's system as the water would flow into the pool. It first builds in the deeper end, where more healing energy is needed, then, reaching the shallow end, the reiki level rises evenly as the water would throughout the pool, as one level surface.

People turn to reiki for all forms of healing, growth, and transformation. I first received reiki when I was seeing an intuitive and spiritual healer on the Lower East Side of Manhattan. I was pursuing acting at the time, and I was looking for natural or alternative methods of coping with my anxiety and emotional stress. A part of me was also lonely and seeking out more of a spiritual community in New York City. No matter how stressed, depressed, hopeless, tired, or negative I felt at the beginning of a session, every time I left my spiritual healer's sessions, I always felt so much more balanced, energized, and upbeat. I became more and more curious and inquisitive about the work, so my healer would suggest books and crystals and other things for me to try on my own time.

I had become disillusioned with the world of showbiz and acting, and felt increasingly pulled toward the idea of offering spiritual healing as a vocation. My healer had a thriving, full-time practice, so it was being demonstrated to me that earning a living as a spiritual healer was entirely possible. At the same time, a part of me was resistant to it, because after years of working freelance and odd jobs to pay the rent, and trying to make it as an actress, the idea of having to build up a whole new business was not appealing to me. I wanted a 401(k), benefits, a stable income, and, yet, my heart kept whispering to me to go in a spiritual direction. So I did. I arrived at my healer's studio one day and announced that I wanted to train and become a healer. She said to me, "I've been waiting to hear you say that, because you have a gift." That was all the confirmation I needed. The next day I picked up the phone and registered for my first-degree reiki class, and began my training a month later.

At the time, I was the only one in my class who wanted to pursue it professionally, so you can see how things have changed! Reiki is now practiced in animal shelters, hospitals, shopping malls, spas, rehab programs, and war zones. Wherever and whenever you need the energy to flow for the highest healing good, it will, and it will always seek out the area of greatest imbalance first. Reiki promotes balance by evening out the energy in all living matter.

A BRIEF HISTORY OF REIKI

霊気

Reiki

Many of the stories told about the history of reiki tend to be more allegorical than fact-based, with many conflicting dates, stories, and opinions on who created it, when it began, and how it came to be practiced in the West before spreading worldwide. There are many styles and lineages of reiki, with new schools and techniques emerging as the practice continues to evolve. Traditional reiki is most commonly attributed to Mikao Usui. It is said that the practice of reiki is based on a system of natural healing he devised in early-twentieth-century Japan.

Exactly how and when the system was devised, and its provenance, is shrouded in mystery and controversy. For many generations, the history of reiki was an oral one, and much of it was surrounded in secrecy. I've heard many versions of the story, including a version that Usui was a Buddhist monk, a Christian minister who later earned a doctorate degree in the USA, as well rumors that he devised his own system based on what he learned from the practice of medical qigong. I've also been told that there were teachers of reiki before Usui and that historical evidence backs up that claim. Well, I maintain that all history is in some way subjective, so I've decided to accept the stories I've been told as allegory. Sometimes we learn more from the themes of a story than from the facts it presents. This is a truncated version of the story told to me by my reiki master teacher.

In the early twentieth century, Mikao Usui, a businessman and theologian, began a quest to uncover the source of ancient healing techniques attributed to both Jesus Christ and the Buddha. After much travel and research, he believed that he had uncovered the knowledge, but he did not yet know how to apply it so that he could master the power of healing. He decided to fast and meditate for twenty-one days, in the hopes that being clear both in body and mind, he would be open to receiving his answer. He climbed Mount Kurama in Japan and found a place that faced east. Since he had no calendar, he gathered twenty-one stones and placed them before him. Every morning he awakened before sunrise and threw away one of the stones to keep count of the days.

On the dawn of the twenty-first day, which coincided with the new moon, Usui felt around in the darkness for the last stone. He began to see a flicker of light in the sky that was moving in his direction, becoming larger and larger as it neared the top of the mountain. Although initially scared of what he saw, Usui realized that it was the sign he had worked so hard to receive, so he sat calmly waiting. When the light reached him, it hit him in the center of his forehead. At first, he thought the impact had killed him, but as he opened his eyes, he saw four symbols floating before him. Each symbol translated its use and meaning to him in a vision, and then dissolved. He lost consciousness after the fourth symbol disappeared, only to reawaken later in full daylight, feeling strong and rejuvenated, despite his long period of fasting.

After discussions with his friends and upon more meditation, Usui decided that he must go to the Beggars Quarter of Kyoto, where he felt compelled to help heal the poor and sick. He spent years devoted to his charitable work, only to realize that he had made a terrible mistake: By giving reiki freely to all those who had asked, he had helped them heal in body, but not in spirit. Time and time again he would see the same faces, requesting healing without making the necessary changes in their lives to improve their health and well-being. By giving away the healing for free, he felt that he had only confirmed the beggar lifestyle, rather than helping to free the people from their mind-sets of ill health and poverty. He concluded that only through fair exchange would there be a value assigned to reiki healing, and that only through the addition of spiritual practice and teachings could the mind and spirit be healed along with the body.

At that point, Usui developed his five reiki principles, still taught as part of the traditional reiki lineage to this day:

> Just for today, do not worry.

> Just for today, do not be quick to anger.

> Earn your living honestly.

> Honor your parents, teachers, and elders.

> Show gratitude to all living things.

These five principles created significant changes in subsequent healings he performed. The new teachings provided spiritual concepts to be integrated and practiced by his patients, along with the healing benefits of reiki. One afternoon, Usui lit a torch and went walking in Kyoto. When he was stopped and asked why he was carrying a lit torch in the middle of the day, with the sun shining so brightly, he replied that he was searching for people who were seeking the true Light. He invited the people to come and hear about reiki. He started teaching reiki throughout Japan and built a following of sixteen master teachers.

Shortly before his death, Usui passed on the lineage of reiki to his greatest friend Chujiro Hayashi, an ex-naval officer who is believed to be the last reiki master trained by Usui. Hayashi developed the three degrees, or levels, that make up the teaching of reiki. Following his first training, Hayashi left the Usui School and opened his small clinic in Tokyo, which had eight beds and sixteen healers, and where practitioners worked in pairs of two to a bed, giving treatment to patients.

There, Hawayo Takata, a lady suffering from a serious illness, was treated and recovered. Impressed by the results, she asked to learn reiki but was at first turned down because, having traveled from her home in Hawaii, she was considered a foreigner and was also a woman. She persisted, and in the spring of 1936, Mrs. Takata received her first degree in reiki. She continued to work with Hayashi for another year and then received her second degree. Takata then returned to Hawaii in 1937, where she was soon followed by Hayashi, who came to help her establish reiki in the West. In the winter of 1938, Hayashi initiated Takata as a reiki master. Hawayo Takata was the thirteenth and last reiki master Chujiro Hayashi initiated. Between 1970 and her death on December 11, 1980, Takata initiated an additional twenty-two reiki masters to the Usui lineage.

The original twenty-two teachers have since taught countless others. In the decades following Takata's death, reiki has spread rapidly in the East and the West and is now practiced almost everywhere. There are now tens of thousands of reiki master teachers and millions of people practicing reiki worldwide.

THE SACRED REIKI SYMBOLS

I was taught that in traditional reiki there were four original symbols: The symbols were considered sacred by the reiki master teachers and kept secret from all those who had not been attuned to them and formally trained as reiki practitioners. The symbols are believed to be transcendental, as they access the source of reiki directly and affect how it flows and functions. This is why so many teachers insist that you need to be attuned to a particular reiki symbol to effectively use it: The power is not so much in the symbol itself, but in the energetic link that is created between the reiki source and the symbol when you are attuned to reiki by a master teacher. They are based primarily on Japanese Kanji, although some of them are fused with Tibetan Buddhist, Sanskrit, or Chinese writing and symbology.

The symbols are activated when you draw them and then say their names out loud three times. They work with form (yantra or calligraphy) and sound (mantra). By drawing the symbol and repeating the name three times, you create a vibration that impacts our physical and nonphysical reality. They are thought-forms that increase and direct the reiki flow, and while the power of intention is undeniable, the symbols are connected to Universal consciousness. Once attuned to them, you need not believe in them for them to work, and your connection to them lasts a lifetime.

I have found over the years that how the symbols are drawn, or even spelled, can vary in style. It is said that Grand-master Takata was known to draw them differently over time to suit different students.

You can draw the symbols with the eyes open or closed and using:

> **THE PALM OF THE HAND**

> **THE BREATH**

> **THE FINGERS**
  (middle and index)

> **THE THIRD EYE ALONE**
  (drawn or visualized as a whole)

Visualize a symbol as you draw it. I always see symbols in etheric form as a non-color, but you can visualize any color that feels right to you. Then invoke the symbol's power by saying its name three times quietly under your breath. The invocation fully activates the energy vibration of the symbol.

Cho Ku Rei, a symbol for power and healing

Sei He Ki, a symbol for balance and harmony

Dai Ko Myo, the master symbol

Hon Sha Ze Sho Nen, a symbol that bridges distance and time

USING
THE SYMBOLS
IN CRYSTAL
REIKI

I found that the more I incorporated crystals into my session work, the less I felt called to use the symbols. Rather than altering and/or affecting the function of the reiki flow with a symbol, I could use a crystal to deliver the specific kind of energy my client needed. For example, I could draw a reiki symbol to help bring calm to a person's system, or I could use blue lace agate, angelite, lithium quartz, petalite, or lepidolite, depending on the underlying cause of the stress. If a client was struggling with empowerment issues, I could place ruby, garnet, and carnelian on her root chakra or at her feet and in her hands. The use of crystals cancels out the need for most of the symbols, with the added benefit of being able to address more than one issue at a time, due to their varying properties and how their energies blend together as a whole.

There are still some symbols, not all of which are considered to be traditional reiki symbols, that I like to work with because they help to open and close a session, provide added grounding or aura healing, and can help to move or dissolve blocked or stagnant energy quickly and effectively.

CHO KU REI

KEY WORDS

Power, empowerment, masculine energy,
activity, yang. It is more physical in its application
than the other symbols.

CLOCKWISE:

PUSHING energy

COUNTERCLOCKWISE:

PULLING energy

> **Can be used to increase the power** of reiki flow.

> **Drawn clockwise, it can empower**, charge, or direct energy, and
> provide energy protection, and can also be used to seal in and
> protect a person's aura or space.

> **Drawn counterclockwise, it pulls out** and removes blocked,
> stagnant, or negative energy, and can relieve pain and disease,
> or release pent-up emotions.

RAKU

(NON-TRADITIONAL)

KEY WORDS

Completion, release, inner peace,
freedom from illusion,
severing of unhealthy connections

> **Can be drawn from the feet up along the body** to help a client connect with his higher self and wisdom; raise his frequency; or, in hospice situations, ease a client's transition.

> **Can be drawn from the top of the head down to the feet** to help a client feel grounded and centered in his body.

> **Can be used in a healing session to sever psychic cords** or unhealthy attachments, as well as to sever the psychic bond or connection formed between practitioner and client at the end of a session.

TIBETAN DAI KO MYO

(NON-TRADITIONAL)

KEY WORDS

Divine light, deep healing, transition, freedom, bliss, empowerment. This is a variation on the original dai ko myo, said to be created or first channeled by Takata.

> **Is equally as powerful as the traditional dai ko myo,** but is less structured and quicker in its effects.

> **Can be used to begin the attunement process** or at the start of a healing session by drawing it into your client's crown chakra to send light down into the body.

> **If drawn into the crown, heart, and root chakras,** can ground the spiritual self in the physical experience.

> **Can be used to help remove illness,** viruses, pain, blocked energy, psychic cords, or spiritual parasitic attachments to the aura.

> **Will open a client's crown chakra** if drawn on the top of the head to increase her spiritual growth or evolutionary process.

> **Can help to support or accelerate healing** in any part of the body.

WHAT IS CRYSTAL HEALING?

Simply put, crystal healing is intentionally working with crystal energy to positively influence our own energy to the benefit of our health and well-being. There are as many methods of crystal healing out there as there are people working with crystals, and their application or uses are limited only by your imagination.

Styles of crystal healing and beliefs about crystals can be found in many cultures, whether indigenous, historical, modern, Eastern or Western, all around the world, and they range from superstitious, to folkloric, to fully developed systems of healing. In the western hemisphere crystals rose to popularity in the 1970s through the 1990s as part of the new age movement, thanks in part to the work of writers and mystics like Katrina Raphael, Uma Sibley, Michael Gienger, Melody, and others. But the healing and metaphysical use of crystals began a very long time ago.

THE
HISTORY
OF CRYSTAL
HEALING

It may surprise you to know that belief in the healing and spiritual powers of crystals is not a new age thing. It's actually a very old thing, as in an ancient old thing. Crystal beads and carvings, believed to be used as talismans (a charm meant to bless the bearer with power or luck) or amulets (a charm meant to bless the bearer with protection), have been found dating as far back as thirty thousand years in Paleolithic gravesites discovered in Europe.

The earliest recorded use of crystals to date comes from the ancient Sumerians, who used crystals in magical formulas. In the epic poem *Gilgamesh*, the Sumerians so valued lapis lazuli that they used it to fashion into ornaments, offer bowls as gifts to the gods, and make commemorative statues of the dead. These lapis lazuli items indicated wealth and power as well as spirituality that represented death, mourning, and the realm of the spirit. Ancient Egyptians used crystals primarily for protection and for their health benefits, wearing them in the form of jewelry. They would also pulverize them, and use them as healing tonics and beauty powders, as well as for grave amulets. Favored gems included lapis, turquoise, carnelian, quartz, malachite, and emerald.

The ancient Greeks ascribed many healing and metaphysical properties to crystals. Theophrastus (372–278 BCE), a famous pupil of Aristotle's, wrote a treatise titled "On Stones," considered to be the first significant work on minerology and geology. It formed the basis for some of the work by Pliny the Elder, who wrote at length about the properties of many crystals and stones in his *Natural History*, an ancient encyclopedia of the natural world.

Many gemstone names can be traced back to their sources, and often are indicative of the metaphysical properties assigned to them. For instance, amethyst comes from the Greek *amethystos*, meaning "not intoxicating" or "not drunken." A wine-colored gem, it was believed to help ward off the effects of alcohol, and was worn as an amulet when drinking.

Hematite, from the Greek *haimatites lithos*, meaning "bloodlike stone," is used for healing blood disorders, and improving the healing flow of blood to injured parts of the body.

Sapphire is a trickier one: In ancient times it's believed that the word *sapphire* actually referred to the stone that is known today as lapis lazuli, but it has been suggested by some linguists that the origin of our modern word *sapphire* may have come from the Sanskrit *sanipriya*, meaning "precious to Saturn." This is interesting because of blue sapphire's tendency to evoke saturnine qualities, such as order, restraint, and wisdom.

Aquamarine, originating from the Latin words meaning "water" and "sea," was carried by sailors as a form of sympathetic magic; they believed it would keep them safe at sea.

Jade, derived from the Spanish *piedra de (la) ijada*, means "stone of colic or pain in the side," a condition it was believed could be healed by jade in both ancient Chinese and Mexican cultures. Jade was highly valued in China. It was used in burial masks, armor, wind chimes, sacred objects, even jewelry and hair combs for the nobility. A similar value was placed on jade in the Mayan and Aztec cultures.

Keep in mind that cultures from all over the ancient world, of different faiths, religions, and healing practices, and, in some cases, separated by thousands of miles, believed in the metaphysical and healing properties of crystals. Crystals are mentioned repeatedly in the Bible, as well as other sacred and religious texts and scriptures, and their use for metaphysical and healing purposes in the West continued through the Renaissance. A number of treatises were published during this time, extolling the healing virtues of crystals, most notably the works of Hildegard von Bingen, a twelfth-century

Benedictine abbess of the Rhineland, who describes the many healing properties of precious gems and metals.

With the Renaissance came a strong shift toward the sciences and the powers of individuals. Beliefs in metaphysical forms of healing were publicly ridiculed and dismissed, but not forgotten. They persisted in mythology, superstition, art, occultism, and folklore, until reemerging into public and private consciousness in the nineteenth and twentieth centuries. Our current practices and systems of healing, involving the laying on of stones, may be relatively new, but they are steeped in ancient lore, study, and history.

THE MODERN PRACTICE OF CRYSTAL HEALING

While the use of crystals, metals, and stones for healing may be ancient, many of those practices and philosophies have been lost to time. Modern practices are based on different theories and beliefs with regard to the function and design of the human body, both in its physical and veritable form (meaning it can be measured by scientific methods), as well as in its energetic or subtle form (meaning it cannot be measured by scientific methods).

There are no standards for crystal healing. It is a diverse, nondenominational, multicultural, and holistic form of healing that is independent and unregulated. This can be a good thing and a bad thing. While many crystal healing practitioners may be steadfast in their conviction with regard to their systems, styles, and opinions on crystal healing, there is no one true way or method. It is largely intuitive, but a growing body of scientific theory, experience, and wisdom supports it. Westerners can feel very attached to the scientific explanations of things, but as I recently explained to my crystal healing students, using herbs as an example, if you ask a Western herbalist how an herb heals, he may give you a scientific, chemical, or biological explanation. If you ask an Eastern herbalist the same question, he might give you an explanation based on Vedic, traditional Chinese medicine, or another holistic healing method from his culture. If you ask a Peruvian shaman how the herb works, he'll speak to you about the spirit of the plant. Who's right? It's simply a matter of which perspective you choose to espouse.

THE SCIENCE OF CRYSTAL HEALING

I'm often asked for a scientific explanation as to how crystal healing works. Truthfully, that's never meant much to me. Perhaps I can't call my years of crystal notes and documented results from crystal heal-ing "evidence," but it was all the evidence I ever needed. However, I have intuitively experienced or understood certain phenomena that I've since sought to articulate in scientific terms to make it easier for others to grasp. After all, I love a curious mind, and there are so many different ways we can learn more about the magic of this world! The important thing to note is that any scientific explanation of crystal healing is, at this time, pure conjecture or theory. In time, I'm hoping that science will be more open to investigating and studying this form of energy healing objectively. In the meantime, here's my explanation.

All matter is energy. At an atomic level, everything is a collection of atoms, made up of empty space, a nucleus containing protons, and neutrons, and electrons that orbit around the nucleus. According to particle theory, all matter comprises subatomic particles that are always moving, vibrating in varying directions, speeds, and intensities, and can only interact with matter by transferring energy. When energy is transferred from one particle to another, it generates waves that can either have a constructive influence, by creating other waves, or a destructive influence, by canceling each other out.

The oscillation or vibration of waves (or particles in "wave mode") charges the electrons orbiting the nucleus, which then creates an electronic field. That electronic field can also generate a magnetic field. Interestingly, the human heart emits an electro-magnetic field that is sixty times more powerful than that of the brain. Science has proven that our bodies do, in fact, generate energy at a cellular level.

All matter vibrates, and frequency is the periodic speed or cycle of that vibration. Everything in the universe has its own unique set of frequencies. These vibrations and frequencies either share or influence energy. People vibrate at varying levels and frequencies, and so do crystals. When a person is in good health, it is believed that she is vibrating at an optimal level, or frequency. When she's in poor health, she's not. Her vibrations are not in harmony and are disrupting her physical functioning. Energy healing with crystals involves exposing a person to a crystal's energy vibrations and frequencies, which, on a particle level, transfers energy that can either create or disrupt, heal, or throw us out of balance.

Likewise, when a person is exposed to harmful external vibrations or frequencies, it can disrupt his internal vibrations, throwing them out of balance or resonance, and bringing on ill health. This is how psychic attack, negative energy, and veritable forms of energy, like electricity and microwaves, can be harmful. Our internal vibrations rely on resonance for homeostasis and balance. One particle will vibrate at the same natural frequency as another, or will be forced into vibrating at that same frequency. When our systems are healthy and functional, they are entrained, meaning that their vibrations and frequencies are in sync with each other.

Entrainment is another way we can influence health and well-being with crystal energy. Entrainment is achieved when there is resonance between two similarly vibrating energies. If we're seeking to restore resonance to a certain part of the body, mind, feelings, or spirit, we can work with crystals that resonate on similar frequencies. For example, a crystal that emits calming frequencies can be used to help entrain a panicked mind to become calmer. The crystal has a similar vibration as the thoughts or state of mind we're seeking to achieve. For entrainment to work, the crystal must have a stronger external vibration so it can force or move the vibration of the thoughts out of their dissonant vibration. This is why it is vital that a crystal be cleared and charged before being used in crystal healing. The techniques for clearing and charging crystals will be discussed in Part 2 of this book.

To sum it up, every part of our physical and energy selves vibrates at certain frequencies, and so do crystals. We can work with the vibrations of crystals that are resonant with the states we're seeking to achieve by entraining our vibrations with theirs, or we can work with crystals that can transfer the energy we need to positively impact our systems.

MY
SYSTEM
OF
CRYSTAL
HEALING

In some systems, practitioners believe that crystal energy should only be applied to the aura, while in others practitioners use crystals to influence the energy meridians, or other energy channels of the body. A few systems encourage practitioners to place crystals only in the immediate space around a person, while in many others practitioners will place them on the body in relation to the chakras. I've had successful experiences doing all of the above.

I developed my system of crystal healing while I was recovering from a very dark and difficult time in my life. I'd lost my job, my health was a mess, I was coping with a family crisis, a guy had broken my heart, and I felt very, very lost. It was then that I was first drawn to crystal therapy, enticed into working with crystals by their magic and promise of healing. People will often remark on my "encyclopedia-like" recall of the various properties and qualities of any given crystal.

For me it's like remembering foods you've eaten: Once you've had pizza, you're unlikely to forget what it tastes like. Because I experienced the energy of so many crystals on a daily basis for so long, and observed their effects, I'm able to remember them and refer to their use when needed. Memorizing the thousands of metaphysical and healing properties of crystals is a daunting proposition, to say the least; it's much easier for you to learn if you simply work with them on a regular basis and pay attention to what you feel and experience from them.

I was also experimenting with crystal healing layouts on my body and my chakras throughout that time. A crystal healing layout is a placement of crystals on the body with the intention of positively affecting your energy to help improve your health, life, well-being, or to support you in your healing or transformative process. I decided to use the Hindu seven-chakra system as the basis of my work, because it seemed to me to be a comprehensive road map of the energy body that could be effectively used when working with crystal energy.

I'd start by setting an intention for my crystal healing session, select the crystals I felt guided to use, and place them on the relevant chakras on my body. I'd lie there for anywhere from 5 to 45 minutes and let the energy of the crystals flow through me. Sometimes I'd have transcendental experiences, or have an emotional release, see visions or feel movement in my body. At other times I'd simply fall asleep.

Afterward, I'd record everything I'd experienced, how I felt, the intention of the session, and the crystals I used, and would make note of any results I had throughout the week. From this body of work I began to integrate the two healing systems—reiki and crystals—by adding crystals to my clients' chakras before starting their reiki session. My clients loved the addition and began specifically requesting the combined Crystal Reiki service, while recommending it to their family and friends. They had enjoyed the calming effects and the nurturing feel of the reiki, but, with the addition of the crystals, we could begin to address their other healing and wellness issues more specifically and with greater success. The combination gave my work an edge, and significantly enhanced—and, in some cases, accelerated—my clients' healing processes. My business and reputation grew, as did the success rate of my work.

Slowly but steadily, my system of crystal healing evolved, as I continued to practice on myself, and to apply what I was learning to my client sessions. I developed a complex system that calls for building a crystal matrix, or pattern, on the body, involving the placement of multiple crystals on the seven main chakras and the minor chakras in the hands and feet. It also included the application or movement of specific crystals through the aura to influence the four main auric layers, or subtle fields, for healing, protective, and energy-clearing purposes.

I worked with the crystals in four principal ways: to dissolve blocked energy (which typically results in symptoms of pain), to increase the flow of chi through the body (increasing vitality, and enabling clients to move through stagnation), to channel positive energy into the body that was needed for healing (love, optimism, passion, calm, grounding, etc.), and to remove any energy from the system or aura that no longer served (like stress or negative vibes).

THE COMBINATION OF REIKI AND CRYSTAL HEALING

Despite my growing focus on the crystal element of my healing work, I always remained committed to the inclusion of reiki. Why? Because reiki and crystal healing make a beautiful pair. By offering Crystal Reiki, I could work with the crystals to specifically address a multitude of issues, but then I could channel reiki to help harmonize all the various energy vibrations, restore balance and overall vitality to a client's system, and help her feel nurtured and relaxed. I also noticed that when I was giving reiki to a client I was better able to be in tune with her energy and the healing process as it was unfolding, and to receive intuitive or healing guidance that I could relay to her after the session if she was open to hearing it.

While there are many reiki practitioners who happily remain within the strictures of a traditional reiki practice, there are also plenty of healers who branch out and combine different modalities with reiki in their sessions, including the use of crystals, essential oils, massage, acupressure, sound vibration, shamanic techniques, even manicures, pedicures, and facials! With crystals, the application is usually intuitively based on the healer's selections and placements of the stones. The problem is that, unlike with reiki, where they say you can never do harm, you can do harm with crystals. It's important to have a well-developed understanding of crystals, their energy, and how they interact with and affect the human body and energy system to safely use them during your sessions.

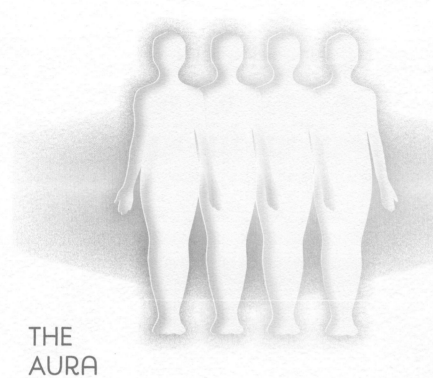

THE
AURA

Crystals can affect every part of our energy body, both veritable and subtle, on a physical, emotional, mental, spiritual, and auric level. We have two energy fields that surround and interconnect with our bodies. The first is a veritable biofield: This is our electromagnetic field, which is generated at a cellular level in our bodies. The second is a subtle field, which is commonly referred to as our aura, and is the etheric blueprint of our bodies and souls.

There are many theories about the aura from cultures the world over, though most of them bear some similarity to the others. Clairvoyants see the aura as a series of bands or layers that surround and interconnect with the body and with the body's subtle channels, fields, and organs. These layers have colors and their own unique frequencies as they graduate out from the body. These colors often represent our state of mind, health, and well-being. Each layer and color is associated with a different chakra, and connects with different realms or energy planes.

The Subtle Fields or Layers of the Aura

THE PHYSICAL RED in color, associated with the ROOT CHAKRA. It is the lowest in frequency of all the layers. The physical field is closest to and regulates the physical body.

THE EMOTIONAL ORANGE in color, associated with the SACRAL CHAKRA. The emotional field regulates our emotional state of being and feelings.

THE MENTAL YELLOW in color, associated with the SOLAR PLEXUS CHAKRA. The mental field processes and filters thoughts, ideas, and beliefs.

THE ASTRAL GREEN in color, associated with the HEART CHAKRA. The astral field is the connection or nexus between the physical realm and the spiritual. It interacts with the causal plane (our physical time /space reality), yet it exists outside of space and time.

For the purposes of Crystal Reiki and the scope of this book, we'll be looking at the first four primary layers, or subtle fields, of the aura: the physical, emotional, mental, and astral.

While each layer or field appears to be outside the body, they also exist within and through the body. It can be helpful to picture ourselves as a series of fields, interconnecting and interacting, rather like colors in a kaleidoscope, when seeking to grasp how our auric fields both reflect and impact our various levels of health and states of being. These fields also represent the different layers of our natural energy defense system.

Crystal Reiki and Healing the Aura

With Crystal Reiki we can address the health of the aura and its subtle fields in two primary ways: (1) by placing crystals on the body and channeling reiki through the crystal into the associated chakras, or (2) by moving crystals through the aura and channeling reiki into the auric fields.

When it comes to matters of physical, emotional, or mental health, you can work within the subtle layers of the aura if you have the psychic means of seeing or sensing them, or you can work on the associated chakra(s) when seeking to affect the energy of a field. Unless you're a clairvoyant or trained in sensing the layers psychically, you may not be able to distinguish the difference between the various layers of the aura, see the colors, and intuitively understand what they mean. But never fear! By looking at a basic chakra diagram, you can see where the associated chakras are situated in a person's body, and you can work on that chakra knowing that the energy will also flow to its associate field. An explanation of the chakras and their functions can be found on pages 32–49.

Every spring and fall I would see clients who were stuck in a cycle of catching cold and flu viruses, never fully recovering from one before they were hit with the next. Their immune system had become compromised or weakened, and it would show up in the physical layer of their auras, which would feel weak, porous, and floating very close to their bodies. That field is connected to the root chakra and is tied to the immune system and the health of the physical body. Along with using crystals on their bodies to help them heal and bolster their immune system, I would also pass a healing crystal through their physical field and then channel some reiki into it. This would help to revitalize and strengthen that part of the aura, helping to ward off the energy of illness and providing added support to the body's immune function.

If you're not sure where the physical field is in your client's aura, you can place additional crystals and channel reiki into the root chakra, knowing that the energy will spread into the physical field. That holds true for anything that might be affecting the emotional field (sacral chakra), and the mental field (solar plexus chakra) as well. You can place healing crystals and channel energy into those chakras, knowing that it will spread into their connected fields.

When it comes to spiritual health and well-being, however, I've found it's imperative to work in the aura with crystals and reiki, as well as applying them to the associated heart chakra. This is because the astral field of the aura, which regulates our spiritual well-being, is a nexus or connection point between our plane of reality and the etheric plane, or nonphysical reality. While the source of a spiritual issue could very well be within our bodies or based in our souls, there can also be causes from the etheric plane outside of ourselves that are causing a problem. If so, the spiritual field will need to be cleared and its energy fully restored to completely resolve the issue.

Here's an example of what I mean: Lucy, a beautiful contralto in a city choir, had been chosen to sing a coveted solo in an upcoming concert. There was a fellow contralto who was very put out by this, and began to gossip behind Lucy's back, staring at her malevolently at practice, and fixating on the intention that Lucy would fail at the performance and the solo would be given to someone else. Lucy told me that she was feeling tired and irritable for no apparent reason, wasn't feeling like herself, and was having nightmares about that fellow contralto. I suspected that these were all signs and symptoms of a psychic attack, so I checked the spiritual layer of her aura. Sure enough, there were psychic cords (malevolent energy attachments that form between one person and another), lots of heavy energy and psychic debris, and her astral field felt spiky with anger and weak in some places.

The first thing I had to do was clear that negative energy off her astral layer (I describe how to do that in the final section of Part 3). Then I placed healing crystals over her heart chakra while channeling reiki into her aura to help strengthen and repair that field. Fortunately, she felt much better after the session, and aced her performance a few weeks later. If I hadn't cleared her astral layer first, the negative energy in her field would have persisted, continuing to damage her aura and plague her feelings. In some cases the energy may get worse and worse, heavier and heavier, until the poor person receiving it has a breakdown. No deep healing can be achieved if there's malevolent or negative energy damaging the aura.

Ultimately, any physical, emotional, mental, or spiritual imbalance in the body or in the space around you can affect the health of your aura. Other factors may include recreational drug use or addiction, heavy habitual drinking or alcoholism, unhealthy diet or lifestyle choices, severe stress or trauma, psychic attack, curses, spirit attachments, and past-life or karmic wounds. You don't have to be a purist or a saint, but I assure you that if any part of your being is experiencing ill health or harm, it will show up in your aura.

THE CHAKRA SYSTEM

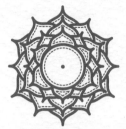 CROWN

 **THIRD EYE**

 THROAT

Chakra is a Sanskrit word that means "spinning wheel of light." Chakras are major energy centers that overlie major nerve plexuses and organs in the body. Chakras have their own unique colors and frequencies, spin at their own particular velocities, and are associated with subtle energy fields in the aura.

 HEART

 SOLAR PLEXUS

 SACRAL

 ROOT

Chakras regulate the functioning of our entire being—the physical, emotional, mental, and spiritual parts of ourselves. They receive energy from the outside world through the fields in the aura, and transform it into energy that can be used by our varying systems, as either subtle energy or as sensory information. This energy is spread throughout the body by energy channels called *nadis*, which function in a similar fashion to veins in the circulatory system, only nadis are delivering a flow energy rather than blood. The vibration and frequency of the chakras allow them to radiate from inside our bodies and spiral outward in both directions. When clairvoyantly seen or felt, they appear to spiral conically out from the front and back of their location in the body, interconnecting with our biofield and the layers of our aura.

The speed at which they vibrate varies by their location in the body: The higher the location, the faster the vibration, and vice versa. The lower chakras vibrate more slowly, are closer to the infrared section of the color spectrum (yellow, orange, and red), and regulate parts of our physical bodies, emotions, and relationships to our physical world. The upper chakras vibrate more quickly, are closer to the ultraviolet colors of the light spectrum (blue, indigo, and violet), and govern our mental, and psychic or spiritual selves, as well as our relationship to each other, other realms, and the Divine.

When any part of our being is imbalanced, diseased, or in a negative state, it affects the relevant chakras and how they behave in terms of color, luminosity or brightness, vibration, frequency, and function. I've heard a lot of people in the spiritual community over the years talking about chakra balancing and aligning the chakras without fully understanding what that means. In my work I've found that some chakras can be stronger than others and that they tend to shift in response to what's happening in our bodies and our lives. Because chakras are energy and energy is always moving, maintaining a balanced system is a matter of daily practice and lifelong choices, as opposed to a net or end result or even an ideal state.

Our chakras do not become balanced because we apply crystal and reiki energy to them. They become balanced when we apply crystal and reiki energy to what is causing them to shift out of balance in the first place, and when we make consistent choices to support their balance. It concerns me when I hear someone say that they "balanced" a client's chakra in a healing session. Did they really? What was causing the chakra to go out of balance? A virus, an injury, fear of abandonment, an addiction, a sexual assault, or childhood trauma? Can you really resolve that and balance the relevant chakra in one session?

It's reasonable to understand that people expect their chakras to be in perfect alignment and proportion to one another, as this is the image so often depicted of the chakras in spiritual artwork. But we are beings made up of diverse, interacting energy fields, all of which respond to our state of health, choices (including thoughts and lifestyles), and our environment. While it's desirable to achieve a state of homeostasis, it's predictable that our various energy systems will be in a state of constant flux. And that's totally OK!

When people refer to aligning the chakras, they typically mean balancing the energy of each chakra so that it is performing at its optimal level. People will also refer to a chakra as being *too open* or *too closed*. I prefer the terms *excessive* or *deficient* to describe the function of an imbalanced chakra. Excessive, or open, means there is too much energy flowing through a chakra, usually as a compensation for a deficiency somewhere else in the system. Deficient, or closed, means there is too little energy flowing through a chakra, usually due to either an excessiveness somewhere else in the system or an energy blockage that's damming up the works. That energy blockage, deficiency, or excessiveness can be the result of any physical, emotional, mental, or spiritual issue.

ROOT CHAKRA

The root chakra is located between the base of the spine and the genitals. It is red and represents the Earth element. It is associated with the physical field of the aura and regulates the physical body. This chakra manages the body's survival needs, including the need for food, shelter, and protection, and basic instincts like procreation and fight-or-flight reactions. Family and tribal (i.e., societal and cultural) relationships relate to and influence the well-being of this chakra. It is relevant to achievements in the material world, permanence, strength of character, patience, endurance, and safety. Related organs and parts of the body are whe anus, the genitals, the bones and skeletal system, the legs, and the feet.

When a root chakra is balanced, we are capable of physical activity, exercise, and taking action to provide for or defend ourselves. We remain grounded and present. We have a healthy and functioning immune system, solid family and cultural relationships, and are able to confidently and consistently meet our survival needs. We maintain good levels of physical endurance, strength, health, weight, and vitality.

When a root chakra is deficient, we experience blocked abundance and provision shortfalls. We have a history or present circumstance of significant family dysfunction, cultural issues, and conflicts. We suffer from a lack of feeling grounded, healthy, or full of vitality. We tend to not be dependable, feel incapable of managing day-to-day obligations effectively, have arousal issues, and will experience physical weakness, weight imbalance, fatigue, and overall malaise.

When a root chakra is excessive, we experience addictive behaviors, like hoarding, hypochondria, and eating disorders. We feel insecure or have a lack of confidence in our ability to survive in the world, and may suffer from unsubstantiated fears of illness or other related survival fears. An excessive concern about material wealth, status, and ownership of material goods plagues us. We have weight issues and body image issues, never feel safe, and have frequent bouts of diarrhea or constipation with no obvious physical cause.

SACRAL CHAKRA

The sacral chakra is located in the lower abdomen, below and behind the belly button. It is orange and represents the water element. It is associated with the emotional field of the aura, and regulates our emotional selves and experiences. It is the source of our creative and emotional energy, desires, and passions, and influences our ability to experience and share pleasure. It supports us in forming healthy relationships with others and in developing our own sense of self and our personality. The sacral chakra regulates our sense of sexuality and sensuality, intimacy, ability to nurture, and desire to be social with other people. Related organs and parts of the body are the sexual and reproductive organs, the bladder, the prostate, the womb, the intestinal tract, and the kidneys.

When a sacral chakra is balanced, we feel emotionally healthy and stable, and are open to meeting new people and forming physically and emotionally intimate relationships. We are friendly, imaginative, and creative, and have a strong sense of who we are in terms of our desires, tastes, and personality. We are fueled by our passions; can physically enjoy our life, body, and physical sensations; and feel empowered. We experience regular and balanced function of our sexual and reproductive organs. We are willing to nurture both ourselves and others.

When a sacral chakra is deficient, we feel blocked in our creative flow, inspiration, and endeavors. We feel unsafe or unable to experience physical and emotional intimacy; suffer from a low sex drive; and feel a significant lack of sensitivity, pleasure, or passion. We're prone to isolationism, and are reluctant or resistant to engage in social interaction. We tend toward depression and being morose. We have reproductive issues, kidney or bladder stones, slow or inefficient digestion, hormonal imbalances, and may experience chronic lower back pain.

When a sacral chakra is excessive, we are prone to addictive behaviors, like sex addiction, alcoholism, drug abuse, or food addictions. We experience frequent and dramatic mood swings, are overly social and in need of companionship, and avoid being alone. We may have scattered creative impulses with an inability to finish what we start, to focus on one thing at a time, or to master any form of discipline. We tend to avoid our deeper or authentic feelings, have regular and possibly intense bouts of anxiety, hyperactivity, and loyalty issues. We have kidney, bladder, digestive, or reproductive inflammatory issues, as well as hormonal imbalances.

SOLAR PLEXUS CHAKRA

The solar plexus chakra is located over the stomach, just below the rib cage. It is yellow and represents the fire element. It is associated with the mental field of the aura, and regulates and processes our thoughts, ideas, and beliefs. *Clairsentience*, the psychic ability to physically and emotionally sense or feel energy vibrations (including emotions), is located in the solar plexus chakra. This chakra, one of our major personal power centers, helps to determine our sense of identity and confidence, our levels of will and ambition, our ability to manifest our destiny and prosper, our determination, and our sense of empowerment. Related organs and parts of the body are the muscles, the stomach, the pancreas, the liver, the gallbladder, metabolism, immune system, kidneys, and the nervous system.

When a solar plexus chakra is balanced, we have a strong sense of self, but are willing to be flexible, open, and teachable in our behavior, beliefs, and choices. We feel empathy and at the same time affirm strong and healthy boundaries with others. We have the energy and determination to pursue our goals and desires, but are willing to let things go when they are not good for us or are not working. We prosper, thrive, and flourish in the world, and have a healthy digestive and elimination system. We manage our stress, feelings, and desires in a way that is balanced and wise.

When a solar plexus chakra is deficient, we consistently feel frustrated, blocked in our desires or endeavors, ill at ease or insecure, and confused about who we are and what we want. We are easily influenced by others and routinely allow our boundaries to be violated (if we're even clear on what those boundaries are). We tend to give up before starting, are self-defeating, and tend to put ourselves down a lot. We may secretly feel envy and spite with respect to the success and achievements of others, and have a fear of conflict. Digestion is slow and sluggish, and we often feel fatigued, overwhelmed, and possibly depressed. We are prone to drug addiction, particularly with opiates, marijuana, and prescription painkillers.

When a solar plexus chakra is excessive, we tend to be domineering, authoritative, abusive, and close-minded in our beliefs. We are insensitive to the needs and feelings of others, and feel overly concerned with our own. While we may be prospering, it is never enough; we always need more and will take more than our fair share when offered (or not). Our temper is quick to flare, and we may frequently violate the boundaries of others. We push ourselves too hard, are too demanding of ourselves and others, and may maintain impossibly high standards that we strive to achieve. We place a premium on social and economic status; we often find ourselves in conflict with others, especially authority figures; and frequently feel wired yet tired. We are prone to having ulcers, inflammatory digestive conditions, acid reflux, and addictive behaviors such as alcoholism and gambling.

HEART CHAKRA

The heart chakra is situated in the center of the chest, just slightly above the heart. Its color is green and it represents the air element. It is associated with the etheric field in the aura, which governs our relationships with ourselves and others individually, collectively, and Universally. The heart chakra enables us to experience, share, and receive love (including higher or divine love), compassion, and forgiveness. It helps us to connect with and sense the essence of nature and to feel more in tune with the plant and animal world. Related organs and parts of the body are the physical heart, the lungs, the thymus, circulation, the metabolic rate, the bronchial tubes, and, in part, the endocrine and immune systems.

When a heart chakra is balanced, we are able to genuinely nurture, love, and forgive ourselves and others, and to have a healthy sense of self-worth. We are better able to live in the present than to be trapped in the painful memories of the past. We are generous but not to a fault; we have healthy emotional boundaries and balanced inter-personal relationships. We are in tune with our feelings and needs, and are willing to honor them as well as respect those of others. We are able to engage in and maintain loving, compassionate rela-tionships with animals and the natural king-dom. We feel secure in trusting ourselves and our decisions. We maintain a good level of cardiovascular health and equilibrium in our internal systems.

When a heart chakra is deficient, we may feel depressed, "heart heavy," tend toward sadness and morose-ness, and be trapped in grief or unwilling to let go of past painful experiences and memories. We may be emotionally wounded, oversensi-tive, and afraid to trust other people or be vulnerable. We may be resistant to developing loving relationships. We are miserly in our choices, feelings, and behaviors, and have trouble feeling compassion or expressing kind-ness to other people and other forms of life. We feel emotion-ally cold and closed off, and frequently experience congestive respiratory or heart illnesses, cancers, and fatigue, and may contract viruses more easily.

When a heart chakra is excessive, we desperately need to feel loved, accepted, and approved of by others in order to have some sense of self-worth. We are very vulnerable to gossip and criticism. We overgive in terms of time, help, charity, and emotional support, often in violation of our own emotional boundaries and to the neglect of our own feelings and needs. We always, always, put other people, things, and obligations first. We feel acute emotional pain when witnessing, thinking, or hearing about harm to animals or the environ-ment, to the point where we're experiencing more of our own pain than that of empathy. Our emotions are triggered very easily and we seek out confir-mation from others, rather than trusting our own self. We are usually too trusting of others. We are prone to heart arrhythmias, heart attacks, stroke, and asthma.

THROAT CHAKRA

The throat chakra is situated in the center of the throat. It is blue and represents the ether element. It governs our ability to express ourselves and communicate with others; to listen to ourselves and others; and to be honest, authentic, and self-aware. It also governs our receptivity to higher guidance, divine messages, and spirits; our ability to manifest our spoken intentions and desires; and artistic creation. It is also the main energy center for the psychic ability of *clairaudience*—the ability to hear and articulate information from spiritual sources—and to channel messages fromspirits in mediumship. Related organs and parts of the body are the mouth, the teeth, the throat, the thyroid and parathyroid glands, the tonsils, and the nose.

When the throat chakra is balanced, we are able to honestly and openly express ourselves, articulate ideas, beliefs, and concepts, and are aware of our own worth, truth, needs, and feelings. We are able to confidently express our needs and boundaries, ask for what we want, and put our creative ideas out into the world. At the same time, we are able to hear the needs and ideas of others, are actively engaged listeners, and are willing to consider what we are hearing. In spiritual work, we often hear guidance as though it had been spoken to us, and are able to listen to our intuition, as well as to cultivate spirit mediumship skills.

When the throat chakra is deficient, we often experience an inability to speak up for our own needs, boundaries, or self-worth, and are afraid to ask for what we want. We are blocked and often repressed when it comes to emotional, intellectual, or creative expression. There's a reluctance and resistance to being heard, being the focus of attention, or being acknowledged, and when called upon to speak we have trouble effectively articulating ourselves. We are never, ever willing to accept a compliment. A deficient throat chakra causes a great deal of self-denial and lack of authenticity, and we are prone to deception, lies, or fibbing, often because we don't feel that expressing our truth is enough. We are vulnerable to congestive throat, nasal, and bronchial issues, as well as tonsillitis.

When the throat chakra is excessive, we feel unable to listen to, hear, or acknowledge what others are saying or their accomplishments. We tend to be domineering or abusive in our relationships, impose our own will, and demand that our needs be met and our feelings understood. We have a strong desire to be the center of attention, are excessively verbal and talkative, and feel the need to express everything we are feeling, thinking, or processing. No filter! We are prone to having tension and soreness in the neck, shoulders, and throat area, and are regularly affected by inflammatory throat issues, strained vocal cords, and physical hearing issues.

THIRD EYE OR BROW CHAKRA

The third eye chakra is in the middle of the forehead. It is indigo or purple and represents the element of light. It regulates our psychic, cognitive, and sensory abilities. It enables us to think both logically and abstractly, function intuitively, as well as learn, remember, visualize, focus, imagine, dream, and understand the difference between fantasy and reality. *Clairvoyance*—the psychic ability to see subtle energy, realms, spirits, time, and space—is governed by this chakra. Related organs and parts of the body are the eyes, the medulla plexus, the ears, the central nervous system, the cerebellum, the brain stem, and the pituitary gland.

When the third eye chakra is balanced, we are able to learn and develop new ideas, languages, and information; grasp new concepts; and see or consider things from different perspectives. Both our long-term and short-term memory capabilities are functional and sharp. We can focus our attention, as well as tune out distractions, visualize with our mind's eye, and intentionally shift our consciousness from awareness to a trance state with ease. We are able to process sensory information that informs us of both our internal and external worlds. Our imagination flows freely, we frequently remember our dreams, and our intuition is clear and strong. We are capable of and open to developing our own psychic strengths and abilities.

When the third eye chakra is deficient, we feel that our intuition is blocked or have trouble distinguishing between our intuitive guidance and our fear-based inner voice or dialog. We have trouble feeling inspired or connecting with our imagination, and have difficulty remembering our dreams. We may experience challenges in learning, remembering, and processing new cognitive or sensory information. We often have a limited perspective and experience an inability or unwillingness to change our perspective, see things from a different angle, consider new or alternative possibilities, and understand another's position or viewpoint. Our thinking can often feel clouded, vague, or unclear. Oftentimes, we develop eye and ear health issues, and experience frequent sinus congestion or infections.

When a third eye chakra is excessive, we have an unduly suspicious nature, questioning other people's motivations, thoughts, and intentions without any basis or provocation. We can be prone to projection of our own issues and feelings onto others, taking things too personally, and being overly absorbed with ourselves and our personal dramas. Frequently, we're unable to focus, and experience a lack of clarity due to scattered thinking and impulses. While our intuition and psychic abilities may feel blocked, we're actually experiencing fatigue with these faculties due to overuse, overdependency, or burnout. We will frequently have headaches, eye strain, or a runny nose.

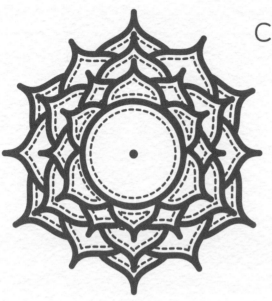

CROWN CHAKRA

The crown chakra is situated at the top of the head. Its color is violet, gold, or white, and it does not represent an element. It is our divine connection to higher consciousness, Christ consciousness, the collective unconscious, God/dess, Great Spirit, or Source, and the Universe as a whole. It supports us in embracing our interconnectedness with all life, and our spiritual self. It governs our access to higher guidance, wisdom, soul-level memory, spiritual beliefs, and our higher self. It influences our ability to have faith, and the religious or philosophical beliefs we choose to espouse. Related organs and parts of the body are the cerebrum, the brain, the central nervous system, the endocrine system and the pineal gland, the scalp, and the hair.

When the crown chakra is balanced, we are able to see things from a higher perspective, as opposed to remaining stuck within our emotional or compartmentalized versions of reality. We have a higher idealism when it comes to the world and human potential. We have access to archetypal, ancestral, tribal, and higher dimensional knowledge and ideas, and can access the Akashic records and past-life memory. We have a sense of or a belief in a higher organizing and creative intelligence, entity, or being (i.e., God), and are open to the beliefs and philosophies of others. We are able to keep our own counsel and maintain healthy psychic and energetic boundaries, despite what others may try to compel us to think or believe. We have a strong and loving sense of ethical responsibility and a steadfast moral compass.

When the crown chakra is deficient, we experience an inability to think for ourselves or trust our own wisdom, beliefs, and convictions. We are easily swayed by the beliefs and philosophies of others, and will often develop a codependency on the authority figures that represent these systems, to the point of embracing a cult or an extreme religious dogma. Our spiritual growth feels blocked or is stagnated, and there is a marked inability to rise above and see the bigger picture as a whole. There is a resistance to believing in a higher power, and an apparent lack of faith. Ethical and moral boundaries are unclear and undeveloped. Physically, we may experience hair-growth or hair-loss issues and headaches.

If the crown chakra is excessive, we feel ungrounded, spaced out, and have trouble managing day-to-day tasks or staying on top of details. There is a general lack of follow-through, a lack of accountability, and the belief that the realm of physical reality is secondary to that of the spiritual, and to our spiritual aspirations. We will frequently express our spiritual, moral, and ethical superiority to others, and hold our chosen beliefs and practices to be the only right and true way or path. We seek to impress our belief systems on others, and to accept any higher or spiritual guidance we receive from the ethers as being true and wise without caution or consideration. Physically, we will often experience headaches, dizziness, or vertigo, and can be prone to developing mental illness.

Part 2

A HEALER'S PREPARATION

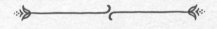

PREPARING
FOR A HEALING

I learned a very hard lesson about healer preparation early in my healing practice. I had transitioned my healing space from my apartment to a rented therapy room in Manhattan. It was only an hourly rental, as opposed to a lease situation, so I had to drag all my things there and back each day (crystal kit, tuning fork, smudge stick, sheets, CDs, etc.). Physically it was hard on me. My crystal kit alone weighed close to thirty-five pounds, and I'd be climbing up and down subway station stairs, lugging that kit together with my bag of supplies, and walking several blocks to and from the building. Once I arrived in my space, I'd have to move around furniture and set up my massage table, all the while hoping I didn't throw my back out in the process. It was a lot of work—I certainly didn't need a gym membership in those days!

Adding to the physical strain was the mental and emotional stress I experienced. I have always been a little punctality-challenged, so I'd inevitably be running late and feeling rushed and upset with myself. I'd get into the space feeling slightly frantic and disgruntled, with very little time to prepare before my first client's arrival. It wasn't the best situation for me, in hindsight, but at the time I hadn't quite built my business up to the level where I could afford to lease my own private, dedicated therapy room. I had to compromise and manage as best I could.

One of my regular clients at the time was a TV star who was highly empathic and was feeling trapped in an unhappy marriage. Her nerves were constantly set on edge by the paparazzi. She was seeing me twice a week to help lower her stress level and learn how to manage her sensitivity through aura clearing and shielding practices.

She walked into the room one day and immediately felt uncomfortable. I admit that I was particularly punctuality-challenged that day, so while I'd managed to set up the furniture on time, I hadn't cleared my own energy or that of the space, and I was still feeling a little frantic. As we sat down and began the consultation, my client confessed that she felt she was taking on my anxious energy, that the space didn't feel balanced, and that she felt trepidation about continuing with the session.

I was taken aback, and, in truth, I felt ashamed because I knew she was right. When a client is lying on your therapy table, not only is she vulnerable to the potentially harmful energy in the space, but she's also vulnerable to your own energy through transference. *Transference* simply means that energy has moved or been transferred from one place, person, or thing to another. There's been a lot of criticism directed toward the reiki community for teaching practitioners that they can never do harm with reiki, which in my experience has never proven true. The reiki energy is light energy, so in and of itself it is pure, but you can pick up lower, harmful energy from a person who's giving you reiki just as easily as you can from sitting beside her on a park bench or sleeping in bed with her at night. I had taken for granted that the reiki energy would be clear and that the crystals would do their thing, but I had neglected to consider the deleterious effects that my own energy and that of the space would have on my client.

She went ahead with the session, but left still feeling anxious and unsettled, and, of course, I never heard from her again. It was a big, big lesson to me in terms of the integrity of my practice. It's not enough to have your crystals cleared; the quality of your own energy and that of the space are equally contributing factors in a healing session. If they're not up to par, not only are you diminishing the quality and effectiveness of your work, but you're also risking harm to your client. I made a vow to myself that day that I would never allow that to happen again. And I never did.

From then on, I made sure I showed up early so that I wasn't feeling rushed, I had time to set up and clear my space, and I was ready and in the zone when my client walked through the door. Not only did this contribute to a higher level of quality and success in my healing work, it also led to a more profitable and abundant business. My clients would comment that the second they walked into my space they would start to feel better, and that they felt safe and loved while in a session with me. If you're willing to provide anything less than that standard in your healing work, you need to seriously ask yourself if you're in the right business. Imagine walking into a doctor's dirty office and receiving a jab in the arm from an angry nurse wielding a used needle! No thanks. Ethics, standards, and a high level of integrity in your practice are what distinguish a pro from an amateur, and are part of what makes a healer truly great.

The good news is that maintaining high standards and integrity with your preparation is not complicated. It's a step-by-step process that, if you commit to following it diligently and mindfully, will pretty much work for you every time. Once everything's set up to support you in your work and your client in his healing process, you can relax and let the energy flow. Added benefits typically include an increased ability to channel healing energy, receive clearer and more accurate intuitive guidance, build a prosperous business, and develop long-standing and rewarding relationships with your clients. Win, win, win!

The following sections will guide you through your preparation process, from the beginning through to starting your session.

STEP 1

PREPARING YOUR CRYSTALS

To work effectively in healing, crystals need to be cared for properly. Their energy needs to be pure and strong, and they must be carried and stored in such a way that they won't be damaged, but are still organized and easily accessible to you during your session.

The most important rule in healing work with crystals is that they must be cleared. That means clearing them of any foreign or residual energy (which I'll refer to going forward as "psychic debris") that they've picked up by means of transference from other people and places. Most (but not all) crystals will receive energy as they emit it, so the risk of negative transference between a crystal and your client, or yourself, is very high.

Never work with a crystal without clearing it first, and never ever use a crystal in a healing session without clearing it first. While I'm a great believer that rules are made to be broken, this is not one of them. If you do not honor this, you risk doing harm to yourself and others, and it will directly and dramatically impact the level of integrity, value, and effectiveness of your work in a very detrimental way. Using a crystal that hasn't been cleared is like using a medical tool that hasn't been sanitized.

It's best to begin your crystal prep by clearing your crystals the day before your session, as some clearing methods take longer than others. Then you still have to make sure they're charged (that is, they have strong energy), and are packed up safely or set up in your space and are ready to go. There are a number of different ways to clear your crystals, and it really comes down to preference, practicalities, and time. Again, the most important thing is to be as thorough as possible. In most cases, the methods for clearing crystals are the same as for charging them.

Why? Because, ultimately, what you're doing is increasing the vibration of your crystals, which raises their frequencies, thereby repelling, expelling, or dissolving anything lower that can't match that frequency. Lower, harmful energy and psychic debris typically have a slow vibration and a low frequency, so they simply can't hang around. By raising a crystal's frequency, you're returning it to its natural state, recharging it in the process.

1–3-Hour Methods

The following methods are useful if you have a couple of clients booked into your day, with a few hours in between each, or for any other reason that you might be short on time. They're still fairly thorough, but you may find that after a few rounds your crystals require a longer method to fully recharge and replenish their energy.

> **Place them on a log or a flat slab of selenite.** The important thing here is that the selenite itself is regularly recharged so that it can be thoroughly effective in clearing your crystals. I've found the best ways to recharge your selenite is by either placing it under full moonlight overnight, or setting it among healthy, broad-leafed plants for 24 hours.

> **Wrap them in fresh, green leaves from healthy trees.**

> **Put them in seawater.** Despite the pollution, the diluted salt in the seawater helps to clear and restore crystals.

> **Immerse them in a bowl of freshly collected rainwater.** This stumps a lot of people because of how polluted our rainwater can be; however, the crystals are unaffected by the pollutants. What clears and recharges them are the negative ions in the rainwater. Understandably, this is not something you can have on hand at all times. But whenever it rains, I stick a bowl outside so that some of my crystals can benefit.

> **Expose them to direct sunlight.** *A caution here*: The energy of direct sunlight is highly intense, and can be damaging to a crystal's energy, as well as potentially fading its color. While I've never met a crystal that didn't love moonlight, I've met plenty that don't love the sun. Meteoric-based crystals, like moldavite and tektite, have been an exception to this rule, but overall, I recommend that you experiment before adopting this as a crystal-recharging strategy. Place a crystal in sunlight for 10 minutes, and then hold it in your receptive (non-dominant) hand and see how it feels. If it feels dull, spiky, or weak, keep it out of sunlight. I've had crystals literally crack in half from being left in direct sunlight for too long!

Quick Methods

When I had a full-time healing practice in New York City, I could have as many as five or six clients booked back to back in a day. That's a lot of crystal action! Even though my crystal healing kits were huge and I had at least two pieces of almost every crystal, I'd still be faced with having to reuse crystals throughout the day. That's when these quick methods would come in very handy, I'd use one or two of the following methods in between each client to clear the crystals I was re-using in their sessions:

› **Smudging with sacred smoke.** You can either hold individual crystals and pass them through the smoke or, if you have quite a few to clear, you can place them on a countertop and use a feather wand to waft the smoke over all of them.

› **Expose them to the sound vibration** of a tuning fork or a singing bowl.

› **Use reiki symbols.**

› **With this method you have to clear each crystal individually.** Hold the crystal in your receptive (non-dominant) hand, and then first draw a counterclockwise cho ku rei with your dominant hand to pull impurities out of the crystal (repeat as it feels necessary), and then draw a clockwise cho ku rei to send powerful healing and recharging energy into the crystal.

Overnight Methods

I highly recommend using overnight (or 12–24-hour) methods, as they tend to be the most thorough and result in fully charged, cleared, and happy crystals. Some of my favorite methods are:

> Burying them in uncooked, organic white or brown rice.

> Leaving them to sit beside a healthy, broad-leafed plant (either potted or in your garden).

> Covering them in rich soil.

> Placing them in a bowl or glass of lightly salted water.

> Putting them out under direct full moonlight.

> Placing them at the base of a healthy, full-grown tree. I've found this especially beneficial for metal-based stones, like hematite, pyrite, Boji stones, and so on.

Once your crystals have been cleared and charged, they need to be either packed or stored until use. Again, how you do this comes down to preference, practicalities, and timing, but what worked best for me was to store and carry them in metal makeup boxes that I would buy at department stores. I'd line the interior compartments with either velvet or cotton batting, and then separate my crystals in the compartments based on chakra association. This made it easy for me to find what I was looking for while in a session, and I didn't need to worry about setting them all out on a table somewhere (especially if there wasn't sufficient space in the room). I could just open up the boxes and pull out what I needed.

You can get creative in terms of how you store your crystals. If you have to commute with them, as I often did, make sure you pack them carefully, but not in such a way that it's taking you hours to pack and unpack your crystals, as that's simply not practical. You can wrap them in cloth, put them in pouches, place them in old jewelry packaging, or surround them in bubble wrap. Selenite sticks can be protected by wrapping them in cloth, paper towels, bubble wrap, and the like, and then placing them either in a bag or in a poster tube for extra protection.

If you are able to keep them in a fixed space (like your own dedicated office or therapy room, or a healing room set up in your home), it might be most practical to keep them on a tabletop or on shelves. You can place them on squares of soft fabric, in bowls or shells, on bamboo mats or plates—whatever you feel is nurturing to them. I do not recommend placing them in metal bowls, as metal picks up and conducts energy from a space or a person very easily and quickly, and that could be passed on to your crystals during a healing session, even if they're not being used.

People often ask me if there are rules to grouping crystals. That is, are there crystals that shouldn't be around each other? Are some more harmonious in some groupings than others?

There are no rules, per se; you can group crystals according to color, element, function, chakra, whatever feels best to you energetically and intuitively. That being said, you need to pay attention to how the grouping feels. It's been my experience that high-frequency crystals placed next to slower-vibration, lower-frequency crystals create a dissonance: They generate too many counteractive vibes. The higher-frequency crystals, like selenite or danburite, are shooting energy up toward higher realms, while the slower-vibe crystals, like smoky quartz or bloodstone, are sending energy down toward the Earth. Similarly, I've found that warm, sunny crystals that resonate with feelings of passion, excitement, and activity, as well as the fire element, tend not to jive so well beside blue or cool-toned crystals that are seeking to calm, soothe, and peacefully nurture with their energy.

There are always exceptions, but I find that it's helpful to follow the color spectrum of light or the color sequence of the chakras when grouping crystals: black, gray, brown, red, orange, yellow, gold, green, blue, indigo, purple, violet, white. Pinks can be grouped in with the green, since, in general, they have emotional and healing properties, as well as resonating with many divine love frequencies. You can also group them by element, if you prefer, but given that there are different beliefs and systems when it comes to the classification of crystals and elements, you'll once again need to trust which groupings feel like they emit the best vibe.

Overall, I think the simplest option is most often the best, so I always stick to chakra color groupings with my crystals.

Once you've got your crystals cleared, charged, and organized, next you have to turn your attention to your aura.

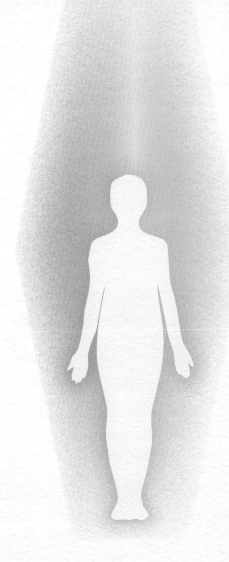

STEP 2

PREPARING YOUR AURA

You need to clear your own aura first *before* physically setting up your room and clearing the energy in the space. People tend to miss this step. Your own energy will affect the energy around you, so you need to clear your own first and make sure it's free of any lower or harmful energy; otherwise, that energy will keep affecting the space you occupy, even as you're trying to clear that space.

Unless you clear your own aura, you could be doing your space-clearing work in vain. Also, before you seek to do any type of energy work, whether it's energy clearing or healing work on your client, it's necessary for your own health, safety, and well-being to be sure that you've cleared and shielded your energy first. This keeps you from taking on any harmful energy from the space or from your client during the session.

The Aura and Psychic Debris

Our auras are made up of electromagnetic as well as subtle fields that surround and move through our bodies. These fields are vital to the maintenance of our health, well-being, and function, as well as a reflection of the state of our health, well-being, and function. A healer's aura is her primary source of energy protection, and defense, as well as one of the means by which she interacts with and affects another being's energy.

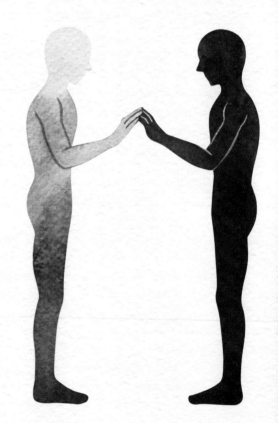

Ever hear somebody say that healers are always getting sick? It's assumed that's because they're always taking on their clients' lower or harmful energy in their sessions, and that assumption is pretty much correct.

I've noticed similar patterns with massage therapists and yoga teachers who get burned out or disenchanted somewhere along the line in their careers. They're taking on too much energy. It doesn't have to be that way, though, if you keep up a daily practice of clearing your energy (and washing your hands!). It's to be expected that in a healing session your energy will be exposed to your client's and the space's, and vice versa. If you're not taking care of your aura, chances are high that you'll take on some of that energy, absorbing it into your subtle fields and chakras. This weakens your aura and energy system, which then makes you susceptible to picking up energy from other places as well, like the subway, the hospital, the grocery store, and the like.

I was considered a "healer's healer" because I became expert at removing that psychic debris from people's systems. Psychic debris can run the gamut from someone else's emotional energy or stress, to dark stagnant energy picked up from a space, to harmful or lower-frequency thought-forms, entities, pathogens, even curses. Furthermore, your own negative thoughts, stress, or emotions, if invested with enough energy, can also contribute psychic debris to your subtle fields, channels, and bodies.How do you know if you have psychic debris in your aura or system?
Here are a few symptoms:

> You feel unusually fatigued, lethargic, or apathetic.

> You don't feel like yourself.

> You're feeling negative, irritable, or aggravated for no apparent reason.

> You're having headaches, feeling stomach tension, or are having digestive and/or eliminative issues without cause.

> You feel blocked in terms of your intuition and access to higher guidance, can't feel your reiki flow, or are suffering from "brain fog."

The truth is, if you're an empath or an energy healer, aura-clearing practices need to become part of your regular self-care routines, like brushing your teeth and bathing. If psychic debris builds up in your system over time, it can make you more vulnerable to psychic attack, parasitic-spirit attachments, even physical and mental illness or imbalance. We're taught growing up to take care of our physical bodies, but we must also learn to take care of our spiritual bodies.

Apart from your own self-care interests, you also have a responsibility to your business and your clients. If you're carrying around psychic debris, two things are likely to happen when you give your healing sessions: (1) that debris can gum up your reiki channel and block your psychic or intuitive abilities, and (2) some of it will be passed on to your client during the session. This means that your work will be impaired. Not only might you be doing potential harm energetically to your client, but if she doesn't feel good after she gets up from your session, she may not come back. The client suffers, and so does your business.

Ethical concerns also surround this practice. Your clients trust you to take care of them and to do your work with integrity. Once a client's lying on your table, he's very vulnerable, both physically and energetically. It's your job to make sure that he's provided for and protected during the session. And if you've got psychic debris in your aura or if you're in a negative state of feeling, mind, or body, you're also vulnerable. Being in a dark, depressed, anxious, or angry place lowers your frequency, which is like lowering the natural defenses of your aura. And if you've got psychic debris in your auric fields, that can magnify and attract even more lower, harmful energy. This puts you at risk of picking up whatever lower energy your client may be harboring, as well as absorbing energy from the space you're in, or even any darker spirits or energy bodies flying around.

I had a number of clients who were working psychics, energy healers, or massage therapists who sought me out regularly for energy-clearing work. This was because they either weren't clearing their energy regularly or they simply weren't trained in how to do it. For the psychics, especially, this kind of energy clearing was essential; without the clearing work, they couldn't get accurate hits in their readings. I remember telling one client that for all the money she spent on sessions with me, she could have taken a nice vacation somewhere if only she'd kept up with her energy-clearing practices!

I know, our days get busy and life gets in the way. But this is an area of your preparation and practice where it does not pay to skimp. Allowing for enough time in your schedule to effectively clear your aura before and after sessions pays off; failing to do it costs you. It's that simple.

Common Aura-Clearing Techniques

I highly recommend that you wait to clear your aura until you are in your healing space, before your session. This decreases the possibility of picking up any debris between the time you clear your aura and the time your first client walks in, especially if you commute to an office or wellness center. There are a number of different ways you can clear your aura—some more effective than others. Whichever method you choose largely depends on the limitations of your space and your preference.

For myself, I found that smudging with sacred smoke, using a selenite stick, or a sound instrument (like a tuning fork or a Tibetan singing bowl) was most effective, but I have worked in spaces where smoke, sound, or smells were forbidden. If that's the case with the space where you do your healing work, you may wish to use one of those techniques before leaving home, and then a second, permissible technique once you arrive in your space.

Smudging with Sacred Smoke

Smudging essentially means wafting around and through your aura the smoke of an herb, incense, resins, or wood that is sacred to your land. The spiritual and chemical essence of the smoke helps to lift, banish, or remove lower and harmful energy frequencies. Smudging and the burning of incense have been used in ritual and religious services since ancient times, and comprise a highly effective method of clearing your aura.

Make sure you pass the smoke (some like to use a feather wand to help waft the smoke in specific directions) over all four sides of your aura, including the top of your head, under your arms, over the palms of your hands, and by your feet, as well as in between your legs. I personally like to use either dried ceremonial sage or a stick of palo santo to clear my aura. I'd do it before and after my sessions, and would also keep a stick by the door for when I came home. You can never overdo it when it comes to clearing your aura.

A note on incense: If you want to use an stick or a cone of incense to clear your energy, make sure the incense is formed from natural plant matter, as opposed to fragrance. If it's just fragrance (meaning a synthetic or fake chemical compound), it won't work.

Using a Selenite Stick

As far as energy clearing goes, selenite really is tops in the crystal kingdom. It is a form of gypsum that is typically tabular and has striations running along the length that I like to compare to fiber-optic cables transmitting pure light-force energy. Unlike quartz, which directs energy like a laser beam, selenite radiates energy and I've found that its effect doesn't differ between rough, polished, and tumbled varieties. The energy it radiates dissolves lower, stagnant, blocked, or harmful psychic debris, and raises the frequency of all forms of energy vibration.

Begin by holding an 8–16" long, at least ¾" wide stick, and tracing it in a counterclockwise spiral above your head to remove any energy blockages from your crown chakra. Then pass the stick slowly down in front of your body to your feet, repeating with the other three sides of your aura. Make sure to pass the stick under your arms and under the soles of both feet, and hold it in the palms of both your hands to clear the energy in those chakras.

When you do this with attention and intention, the clearing work is very thorough.

Purifying Flame

You can pass a lit candle around and through your aura with the intention of exposing psychic debris and psychic-cord attachments to the purifying effects of fire. This can work in a pinch or if you feel there are areas of your aura that are more heavy or dense than others. But I don't recommend this as a regular practice, as I've found it's tricky and time-consuming to be thorough. Also, bear in mind that candles may be prohibited in some spaces because of fire regulations.

Sound Vibration

I have worked in a number of wellness centers over the years where using sacred smoke or scents (including candles and essential oils) were prohibited. Sound vibration is a wonderful alternative for these places. A strong, clear, high-frequency tone can raise the frequency of your energy, automatically repelling, dissolving, or releasing any lower, harmful vibes. The easiest way to work with a Tibetan (or crystal) singing bowl is to sit on the ground with your legs crossed, and hold or place the bowl in front of you while playing it. The sound vibration will envelope and fill your energy fields. With a tuning fork, strike the fork and point it toward yourself. You can pass it down all four sides of your aura, starting at the crown and ending at the feet if you want to be more thorough. Also, if you have a powerful voice that can hold a tune, you can chant or sing a healing or clearing mantra (my preference is OM MANI PADME HUM, a Tibetan Buddhist mantra). You can go by the feel of it when it comes to sound clearing: Once your energy feels lighter, stronger, and clearer, you're likely good to go.

Reiki Symbols and Dry-Bathing

You can draw both the sei he ki and cho ku rei symbols into your aura and the palms of your hands to help clear your energy. You can also practice reiki dry-bathing, known as "kenyoku." Call in your reiki energy, and then place your right hand on your left collarbone. Draw your hand gently down across your torso to your right hip. Then place your left hand at your right collarbone, and draw that hand gently down across your torso to your left hip. Repeat if you feel that's necessary. Place your right hand on your left shoulder and gently wipe down your left arm to the hand. Repeat on the right side with the left hand. Typically, you'd do this at the end of your session, but you can also do this before the session starts to help clear and center your energy. It's been my experience, though, that if there's a lot of debris in my field, this technique does not effectively clear everything, but it can be combined with other techniques as part of your preparatory practice.

Essential Oil Sprays

You can buy energy-clearing sprays that are made with the essential oils from plants that have energy-clearing properties. Again, this can be a useful alternative if you're in a space that won't allow smoke or if you suffer from respiratory illnesses that make sacred smoke an untenable option. Again, make sure that the sprays are made from the actual essence of the plant, not from fragrance, and that you spray all four sides of your aura, your crown, under your feet and arms, and the palms of your hands. A list of plants and essences that are known to have energy-clearing properties can be found on page 76.

Visualization and Prayer Work

You can visualize yourself surrounded and filled with white or golden light, envision yourself immersed in purifying flame, or recite violet flame decrees or psalms from the Bible to help clear your energy. If this is a regular practice for you, and you are able to invoke the energies effectively, this can definitely work. But if you're not sure, or if you're doing things by rote, it's not something I recommend. You can picture yourself surrounded by light, but unless you're actually pulling in those energy frequencies, that's all you're doing—picturing it. This is also why affirmations, symbols, and visualizations tend not to work for many people. It's important to bear in mind, too, that if your energy is heavy with psychic debris, that can impede your ability to call or draw in higher frequencies.

I've noticed that when people most need to do energy clearing, they often feel the least like doing it. The heavier your energy becomes, the less energy you feel you have to take proper care of yourself. As soon as you start feeling this way, that's a sure sign that you need clearing, pronto. In Part 4: Self-Care for the Healer, I share additional methods and practices you can use to help keep your energy clear and strong.

Oftentimes, healers neglect themselves and put the needs of everything and everyone else first. I often refer to the in-flight instructions before the takeoff of a plane as a perfect analogy of self-care for healers: To help the person beside you in the case of a pressure loss in the cabin, you need to put your breathing mask on first. The same idea holds true in healing: To be able to take care of your client's energy, you need to take care of yours first.

Shielding Your Energy

Once you've cleared your energy, it is wise to shield it. While clearing your aura will naturally raise the frequency of your vibration, which can in and of itself repel lower frequencies, there's still something that can work against you when you're doing shielding work: your shadow self. Your shadow self is the part of your spirit or psyche that harbors your fears, shames, judgments, denials, limiting beliefs, wounds, and sabotaging behaviors—parts of yourself that you refuse to accept or acknowledge, and unconscious, negative programming based on what you learned or experienced as a child. You can clear your energy all you want, but you'll never clear your shadow. It's an integral part of yourself. Ascended masters, prophets, and saints who are said to have transcended the reality of human experience didn't overcome or free themselves of their shadows. Rather, they accepted, healed, and reintegrated their shadow fully with the light of Grace. To my mind, that's what it means to become enlightened or ascendant, when the spirit comes into a full state of wholeness and alignment with the soul.

Most of us aren't there yet, and whenever we take a hit of lower or dark energy, it's found its way in through our shadow selves. The shadow recognized the frequency of that energy as similar to one we harbor inside, and it opened the door. Like attracts like, after all. Whenever something, or someone, triggers a negative or lower-feeling reaction in you, you're being shown an aspect of your shadow self.

When I first started my professional healing practice, I was full of desire and motivation and conviction that I was pursuing my purpose, but I was also deeply insecure. I had fears about being able to succeed in building a full-time practice, doubts about my worth as a healer, and worries about not being good enough or knowing enough. I was working at the time at a spiritual bookstore, and had a coworker who sensed and preyed upon my insecurities. He regularly pointed out where I was wrong, what I didn't know, or mistakes I made, and would put me down or undermine me in a way that made himself sound knowledgeable and superior. It was demeaning behavior, but rather than dismissing it as such, his actions triggered my shadow self because I harbored those insecurities. So I'd vie for his attention and approval, and look for opportunities to question or undermine him in turn, in the vain hope that by changing his opinion of me, my own insecurities would disappear. In truth, this was a dance of shadows, because I was likely triggering insecurities in him as well. Clearly, he found something about me threatening.

Which brings me to my next point about the shadow self: Much of it is illusion, false beliefs we've accepted as truths. I was understandably insecure as I was trying something new, but my fears that I wasn't worthy, smart, or talented enough were unfounded; they were based on childhood traumas and false conclusions. And, of course, I was of no threat whatsoever to my coworker: There's plenty of room for all of us to achieve our greatness. But we all have shadows, and while some things may trigger those shadows while others do not, we all contain every grain of human feeling, potentiality, and experience inside us. Whatever we love about someone else already exists within us; whatever we hate about someone else already exists within us. This is true as much for our radiance as it is for our shadow.

Returning to energy shielding: Whenever our energy field, body, or self is exposed to and influenced by lower, harmful frequencies, it is because either our energy system is weak (meaning the frequency of our vibration is low), or our shadow self is coming to the fore. Now, as I've said, we all have shadows, and we likely have lifetimes of healing and reintegration work ahead of us. But that doesn't mean that we have to be so vulnerable. This is where energy shielding is helpful. Energy shielding essentially means that we've created an extra energy barrier to help protect us from psychic harm. Obviously, this doesn't apply to physical sources of harm, like UV or microwaves, exposure to acidic or toxic sludge, but it does apply to harmful spiritual, mental, or emotional energy.

The key thing with shielding is permission: According to the Universal Law of Free Will, nothing can harm us psychically or in subtle form unless we allow it to. This is referred to as divine authority; we all individually hold sovereignty over our own physical and subtle being. As discussed, that authority can be undermined when our shadow self recognizes a frequency and unlocks the back door, without us necessarily being conscious of it. However, when we have acknowledged the existence of our shadow self, and are mindful of when we're being triggered, we can assert our shield and our dominion with absolute authority. When people practice shielding work, they tend to focus primarily on their radiance and their separation from the lower vibes they're seeking to deflect. But when you practice your shielding work with the awareness that lower vibes also linger within your shadow, you can then assert your authority over your whole self. The shadow is included in part of the package, and no other harmful energies can be permitted entrance.

That way lies the true path of mastery, when you're willing to fully accept and acknowledge your whole self—warts and all. When you can lovingly be in that place, even if it's a practice or you're faking it 'til you make it, that decision strengthens you so that outside forces or influences have far less power over you.

Here are common aura shielding techniques:

Invoking Divine Light

I use the term *invoking* as opposed to *visualizing* because I've learned the hard way that unless you're actually channeling energy, visualizing yourself surrounded by white or divine light very seldom works, especially if your shadow's being triggered. When invoking divine light, you need to imagine and feel that you are pulling that energy in and around you, creating a shift in your subtle fields that creates the protective layer.

Divine light should always feel pure, light, and loving in nature. It comes from God or the Highest Power, and cannot be manipulated or tainted. It takes practice to call it in, but the more you do it with pure intention, the more you'll get the hang of it.

Begin by grounding and centering your energy. Imagine magnetically drawing divine light energy down from the heavens and surrounding your body. "Feel" and "see" the light around you, creating a buffer zone that will dissolve and resolve all lower or harmful frequencies for a full 24 hours. Know that it is so, and let it remain there as you return your attention to the activities of your day.

Invoking the Violet Flame

The violet flame is said to be a gift from God to humankind, believed by some to have been channeled from the ascended master St. Germain. As the violet ray, it is the highest frequency of visible light, and is invoked to transmute the negative effects of karma, and lower or harmful frequencies of energy. While there are decrees, mantras, or prayers that one can recite to invoke the violet flame, I know many reiki masters who invoke it as you would do with white, visualizing surrounding themselves in the violet flame whenever they feel they need additional energy protection.

Essential Oils, Sprays, or Hydrosols

I have sometimes been known to spray rose hydrosol in my aura to help amp up my shield. A hydrosol is the aromatic water that is left over from the steam distillation process of extracting essential oils, so the water still contains some of the plant's vital essence. Rose, anjelika root, yarrow, clove, frankincense, myrrh, rosemary, pine, and valerian root are all plants, resins, herbs, or flowers known to have powerful energy-shielding qualities.

Ways to work with them:

> **Spray them into and around your aura.**

> **Anoint power places and points of entry on the body,** like the soles of the feet, the palms of hands, and the seven main chakras, plus the altar major chakra (also known as the "jade pillow" in TCM, where the spirit enters and leaves the body, located over the medulla oblongata at the back of your head).

> **Imbibe an herbal tea or herbal tincture a couple of times a day.** The effects of the herb(s) will radiate outward through your electrical and subtle fields once they're assimilated. This is an especially good idea if you want to work with valerian root, which has a sweet taste but smells something like a baby's dirty diaper.

Wearing Crystals

Refer to the Table of Correspondences on pages 185–187 for a listing of crystals you can wear to help shield your energy. For energy shielding, it's best to wear these crystals over or near to your heart chakra so that their energy will spread throughout your system, and to the outer layer of your aura. You can pop them in your bra or shirt pocket, or wear them in a pouch hanging around your neck, or as jewelry.

Reiki Symbols

You can draw a clockwise cho ku rei into all four sides of your aura, above and below your aura, and into the palms of your hands and the soles of your feet for protection and strength. You can then draw a raku down all four sides of your aura to immediately ground and transmute any negative vibes coming your way.

Pentagram

The pentagram, also known as a pentacle when used in ritual, is a symbol that has gotten a bad rap. It's commonly mistaken as a sign of Satan and devil worship, a stigma that stretches back to witch hunts and anti-pagan propaganda. The pentagram is an ancient symbol that, when drawn with one point up, symbolizes the power of light and Spirit over the material realm. When a protective circle is drawn around the pentagram it becomes a symbol of protection, and has been used for centuries to ward off dark entities, curses, and all forms of lower and harmful energy. You can draw the pentagram into all four sides of your aura, above your head, and below your feet for shielding.

Equal-Armed Cross

Another often misunderstood or misinterpreted symbol, the equal-armed cross shows up throughout human history in almost every ancient culture, from the Chinese to the Mexican, to the Celtic, to the Hindu. It has represented the four cardinal directions, arms of deities, the center point of the Universe, or the stabilization of the Earth, even in modern road and railway crossing signs! While its applications have been diverse, it has also been used for centuries as a symbol of protection, a ward that repels dark spirits and scatters negative energy to the four corners of the Universe.

You can draw it in your aura, as well as on your solar plexus and third eye chakras with a protective essential oil or with holy water (water that has been sanctified by a priest, or that has been consecrated by the four elements).

STEP 3

PREPARING
YOUR SPACE

Once you've got your own energy needs squared away, you can
shift your focus to your healing space. There are two parts to
preparing your space: (1) the physical setup of the furniture in
the room, and (2) clearing the energy of your space.

I always tackle the physical needs of the space first, because once I've got it all set up, the way I want it, it's done, and I can turn my attention to the subtle needs. Keep in mind that when you move things or furniture around in a room, you can disrupt and shift the energy in there, bringing it closer to or further away from balance.

Basic Setup Requirements for Your Physical Space

Good Ventilation

If you're using sacred smoke to clear the energy of your space, your aura, and your client's energy, where does the smoke go? For the smudging to work, the smoke needs to carry the lower energies and positive ions of the atmosphere out of the room, and preferably outside, where it can eventually become transmuted by weather patterns and the Earth's electromagnetic frequencies. Fortunately, most places where I worked had good ventilation, so the smoke would be carried out, but I still remember once working in a boxlike room that had no windows, and no vents! I quickly realized that I would have to use sound and other clearing methods to be able to effectively work in that space.

Furniture

When doing Crystal Reiki, you need a massage table so that your client can lie down, and you need to be able to move around that table a full 360 degrees. There should be a stool at the head of the table on which you can sit; a side table or counter, where you can place your crystals and tools; a chair for your client; and hooks where coats and bags can be hung. That's the bare minimum. Additionally, I liked to have a second chair where

I could sit and face my client during consultation, and a small table between the chairs where my clients could put their handbags, bottled water, and any accessories they needed to remove before the session.

Soft Lighting

Make sure your healing room has either lighting that's on a dimmer switch, or lamps you can light, instead of bright overhead lighting. And definitely try to avoid using fluorescent lights, which strain the eyes and can also skew your psychic sight. Himalayan salt lamps are a wonderful addition to a space: Not only do they cast a soft, subtle light, but as the salt is warmed, it releases negative ions into the space, which clear and balance energy.

Security

Is your space safe, and is it located in a safe part of town? If you're working from your home, what precautions and security measures do you have in place? Are you isolated where you are? Especially in this day and age, you need to ensure your safety. You never know who's coming to see you for a session for the first time, or how a client may react if he feels triggered, provoked, or challenged by you in some way.

Please, please make sure you are safe where you are doing your work. Try not to work in an isolated place, and if you don't feel comfortable working with people who give off a weird vibe, or who leave you feeling insecure, then don't. Period. Why take chances? Just because you're a healer does not mean you have to be a doormat, suffer abuse, or put yourself at risk while doing your work. Reserve the right to refuse a client if you feel uncomfortable or threatened. Honor your boundaries.

Extras

Some of these might be obvious, especially if you've already been working as a healer for a while, or if you've had some formal training, but it's a list I wish I'd had when I first started my work:

A blanket: When people relax, their body temperature drops, so it's important to always have a light blanket on hand. Being covered with a blanket also helps people feel more nurtured and thus relax more deeply.

A clean sheet: This is used to cover your massage table. When washing my Crystal Reiki sheets and blankets I'd always toss in a handful of sea salt with the detergent to help clear any residual energy picked up from clients.

Two pillows: One is placed under your client's head, and one is for your stool if it's not padded and comfortable. Your second pillow can always be rolled up and used in place of a bolster if you don't have anything to put under your clients' knees.

A small, round bolster: Place this under your client's knees while she's lying on her back on your table to alleviate any pressure on her lower back.

An eye pillow or sleep mask: Your client will be able to relax and rest more comfortably if there isn't bright light shining in his eyes. For sanitary purposes, you can place a tissue on his face first, and then place the sleep mask or pillow on his eyes.

Tissues: Useful in case someone starts crying. Sometimes people will become congested as energy is being released during the session and will need to blow their nose.

Water and clean drinking glasses: Energy work, especially with crystals, is very dehydrating. Most clients are thirsty after a session, and it's important for healers to remain hydrated. I drink anywhere from three to five liters of water a day because of my consistent exposure to crystal energy.

Myrrh essential oil: This is a little trick I discovered when I was working in a center that had a communal bathroom one floor and two hallways over from my healing room. I didn't always have time in between clients to run and wash my hands, and I didn't want to use commercial hand sanitizers. Therapeutic-grade myrrh essential oil is antiviral, antibacterial, and antifungal, and its scent is very subtle. You can rub a few drops between your hands to sanitize them. *Added bonus:* The energetic properties of myrrh help to clear, and are protective against, negative energy and psychic debris, and also help to increase reiki flow through the hands. Rubbing the oil on your palm chakras helps to reduce the risk of negative energy transference between yourself and your client.

Music and candles: Music that's soft, gentle, and instrumental only works best in healing, as it helps both yourself and your client to relax without distracting vocals. Which type of music you choose is simply a matter of preference. Candles can add a nice touch, but be aware of the fact that many people can be sensitive, allergic, or turned off by strong scents.

Matches or a lighter: You'll need this on hand if you're using sacred smoke for energy clearing or to light candles. We'll discuss that in greater detail below.

Cell phone signal strength or Wi-Fi accessibility: Unless you're planning to only be paid in cash, you'll need to be able to process electronic payments with an app or an online payment gateway. You also may need to be able to check your emails and messages in case your client's running late, got lost, or is delayed for some other reason.

CLEARING THE ENERGY OF YOUR SPACE

Whether you're sharing a space with other people or if it's your own dedicated room, you always need to make sure that the energy in your space is as sterile as possible before doing energy work in the space. There are a number of reasons for this. It minimizes the likelihood of negative energy transference between yourself, your client, and any psychic debris lingering in the space. It helps to shield the space against any possible spirit interference or disturbance. It increases the potential flow of healing energy and reduces the effects of any geopathic stress in the space. And in a clear space your intuition will be sharper, you'll have a stronger reiki channel, and both you and your client will feel more comfortable and safe.

Scanning Your Space

Before you begin to clear your space, first step into it, close the door, and close your eyes. Bring your sensory awareness to the air in the space. How does it feel? Heavy, dirty, stagnant? Scan every nook and cranny of the space with your awareness, let your imagination open up and flow. Are you seeing or sensing any dark, heavy spots or patches? Areas that feel murkier or keep shifting compared to others? This information will help you to identify areas that may need extra attention when you're doing your clearing work. If the room has any cupboards or closets, make sure you scan those, too.

Now that you've finished your scan, it's time to clear the energy of the space. Spiritual and healing lineages and schools the world over have developed techniques for clearing and balancing the energy of a space. What I'm sharing below is the method that was taught to me by a mentor, as well as several alternatives I've learned along the way. It doesn't much matter which techniques you choose; all that matters is that the space feels clear when you're done. Be sure to do your work with attention and intention. It's easy for a healer to fall prey to routine and start doing things by rote, without focus. The problem with that approach is that when your energy is not in alignment with your actions, both lose potency and power.

The Power of Intention

If you work with God or a Higher Power, call or invite that presence in first and then your reiki energy. If you work with spirit guides or totems, you can call them in as well. Address the spirit of the space, and set your intention to clear any and all lower, harmful frequencies or pathogens from the space, and to create a safe space for healing work. Once you feel solid in your intention, use one of the techniques below or those taught to you by your school, culture, or lineage.

Five-Step Space-Clearing Technique

This is a thorough method that I recommend you do the first time you work in your room, and on a monthly basis after that if the room is being used regularly. This is a technique taught to me by a multi-disciplinary healer and shaman. Do each step methodically and with care.

You will need the following items:

> A rattle or drum

> A smudge stick, ceremonial sage in a fireproof dish, or a stick of palo santo

> Matches or a lighter

> A feather wand or a hand fan

> A white taper candle and holder

> A bell, a chime, or singing bowl

1. **Begin by scanning your space and setting your intention as described above.** If there is a window in the room, open it a couple of inches. If there's there's a vent, make sure it's working. Open any cupboard or closet doors. Remove any unnecessary clutter and empty the garbage.

2. **Pick up your rattle or drum and,** moving counterclockwise around the room, rattle or drum through the space, spending extra time in the trouble spots or heavy areas that came up in your scan. This helps to shake up or loosen the hold of psychic debris or spiritual pathogens in the space so that they can be cleared in step 3, and so that energy can begin to flow more freely through the space. It also serves to distract and confound any spirit matter that may be present in the room.

3. **Light up your source of sacred smoke** and begin to waft the smoke with your wand or fan, again moving in a counterclockwise direction, through the space. The smoke will carry the psychic debris out of the space, either through the window or through the ventilation system. Extinguish, snub out, or let the smoke dissipate once you have finished.

4. **Now light your candle,** and begin to walk slowly in a clockwise direction through your space. The lit white candle represents purity, divine light, and purifying flame. As you walk, say blessings, repeat affirmations, recite a prayer, or chant a healing mantra. Doing this with feeling and authenticity will help to fill the room with your love and divine light, and charge the energy with your healing intention. Snuff out your candle when you're finished, and save it exclusively for your space-clearing purposes.

5. **Take up your singing bowl,** bell, or chime, and walk clockwise through your space, using it to create sacred sound. The sound of your instrument helps to seal in and sanctify the energy, and invokes benevolent spirits and healing frequencies. Listen carefully to the sound of your instrument: Is it reverberating clearly and strongly through the space? If so, that's a sign to you that the clearing has worked.

As soon as you have finished, close your eyes and once again scan your room with your sensory awareness. How does the air feel to you now? What are you seeing or sensing with your mind's eye? The air should feel lighter, clearer, and there should be no dark or heavy spots coming to your attention. If there are, go back to those places with your sound instrument or, if need be, your sacred smoke, and work to dispel the remaining density. Other signs that the space is clear: Colors and light will appear brighter and the shape of objects more defined, your sound instrument will fill the space and sound clear, and you should be able to breathe more deeply and relax more fully in the space. On a daily basis you can use any of the techniques below to clear your space. You can also substitute one of these for step 3 in the five-step clearing process above, if you wish.

Burning copal or frankincense resins: Light up a small, self-igniting disk of charcoal and place it in a fireproof dish or incense holder. Once the disk is hot, sprinkle some copal or frankincense on the disk, and let the smoke billow and fill the space. Both resins are highly effective at clearing negative energy, and the frankincense has the added benefit of sanctifying and shielding a space. When I was doing professional space clearings in the New York City area, this was my preferred method, as people tolerated the smell better than that of burning sage, and I didn't have to put in as much effort to spread the smoke through the space.

Reiki symbols: You can draw cho ku rei and se hei ki symbols, even the Tibetan dai ko myo symbol, into all walls, the ceiling, and the floor of a room, and then stand inside the doorway of the room with your palms facing into the space, and fill the space with reiki light. Again, you'll have to trust your senses and be very focused as you use this technique. I've had mixed results with this technique. It's not always as thorough as I'd like, so I personally prefer using the techniques mentioned above.

Use a Tibetan or crystal singing bowl or chant a sacred mantra: I remember years ago when the Dalai Lama visited New York City, and gave a speech in Central Park. An hour or so before he took the stage, Tibetan Buddhist monks were chanting and intoning mantras. When I asked about this, I was told that they were clearing and sanctifying the energy of the park. Amazing! You can play a singing bowl or chant a mantra to clear a space: The sound vibrations can break down or carry away lower forms of energy similar to the way sacred smoke does. Just be sure to be thorough, use your senses, and only stop making sound when you feel the space has been cleared.

Burning sea salt: Yes, you can burn salt, sort of. Place a handful of salt in a fireproof dish with a heatproof handle. Pour rubbing alcohol (you can also use rum) over the salt, and then set it on fire. The flame creates a type of vortex or vacuum effect, which draws in lower frequencies, purifying them. Walk the flame through the space as you would with sacred smoke, exposing each area of the room to the flame. I admit that I rarely used this technique, as holding such a large, open flame scared me, but I must say that when I was in a space where this technique was used, I really could feel the difference. In spaces where you can't use smoke, scent, or sound, this is an excellent alternative. Just please don't set anything on fire! You can snuff out the flame when you're finished by placing another heatproof dish on top. The fire will go out when it's burned off all the oxygen.

Essential oils: You can diffuse essential oils or use essential oil sprays that contain clearing properties to clear a space. Bear in mind, though, that the scent must fully infuse the space to be effective, and you need to use therapeutic-grade oils, not fragrances, for them to work. You may need to allow some time for the scent to dissipate before it's comfortable for you and your client to work in the space.

What Happens If You Can't Clear a Space?

I have heard stories about a spirit disturbance or a malevolent influence abiding in a space. Among these are spirits of departed ones, dark elementals, fear-based thought-forms, entities, and demonic frequencies. It could also be that great violence, severe stress, or trauma occurred in the room, and the vibration of that event still lingers.

I remember being called to do a space clearing in a heavily cluttered apartment on the Upper West Side. As I worked through the rooms, I encountered the presence of a departed elderly couple in a far corner of the living room. While the wife was willing to pass into the light, the husband refused. I mentioned this to the current owner of the apartment, and he said he knew of the old couple, having been told of their presence years earlier by another healer. As they weren't causing any disturbance, he was content to leave them alone.

When it comes to working with spirits, you need to stay within your scope as a healer. Sometimes you'll encounter spiritual contracts, curses, dark magic, transdimensional portals, and other forces at work. If you are trained or gifted in this work, you may feel honor-bound and called to resolve the situation for the highest good of everyone (and everything) involved, perhaps by moving them into the light or performing an exorcism. But if you're not, and you feel there's a dark presence in the space that cannot be cleared by the techniques I've specified above, I suggest you do one of two things: Either call someone who's professionally trained to do this work to help you, or leave the space. Beware of the ego that may try to edge you on and encourage you to do work beyond your skill set. You cannot risk harm to yourself or another by continuing to offer healing work there. It's not worth it.

FOLKLORIC SPACE-CLEARING TECHNIQUES

I refer to these techniques as "folkloric" because they're based on herbal and magical practices that have been passed down through the generations. At times you'll be working in a room where you'll need to clear not only the space of energy, but the walls and flooring as well. In this case, you can work with sound vibration, as described above; the sound waves will travel through the walls and flooring, clearing the energy. But you can also use the following techniques:

Salt spray for the walls:
Dissolve one tablespoon of sea salt in one cup of hot water, and then pour the mixture into a spray bottle. Spray down all the walls with the salt solution. The salt should be well dissolved and not leave a residue, but if you find one builds up over time, you can give the walls a quick wipe down with a damp cloth afterward.

Herbal floor wash:
Place the juice of two lemons and five to ten drops of pine or cedar essential oil in a bucket of warm water, and mop the floor with the mixture, allowing it to air-dry.

Herbal carpet cleaner:
Grind two dried lemon peels and two tablespoons each of dried rose petals, lavender buds, thyme, and mint. You can grind them in a mortar and pestle, or you can make things easier for yourself and buy a cheap coffee grinder just for this task. Mix your herbal blend with half a cup of baking soda, sprinkle the mixture over the carpet, then vacuum. The mixture will pull up any residual lower energy that's trapped (or hiding) in the carpet.

Crystals for Space Clearing

You can use the following crystals and crystal placements as energy purifiers in a space. Make sure you clear and recharge these crystals once a week to once a month, depending on how often the room is used for healing. **PLEASE NOTE:** You'll still need to practice various energy-clearing techniques in your space, but using some of the crystals below will result in your having to do far less work, less often. You can also refer to the Tables of Correspondences starting on page 185 for a listing of crystals with energy-clearing properties.

You can use the following crystals and crystal placements as energy purifiers in a space. Make sure you clear and recharge these crystals once a week to once a month, depending on how often the room is used for healing.

Selenite: To help purify energy coming up from the street or from neighbors, you can place selenite sticks along windowsills. You can also put selenite towers (a minimum of 10" tall) or pyramids in the corners and center of the space. You can place a log or a large sphere of selenite under your healing table as well.

Calcites: Calcites of all colors gently buffer and purify energy. You can place large chunks of calcite through–out your space to help clear the energy. You'll need to use your sensory awareness to determine specific placements and how many you need, as the energy frequencies of one room will differ from those of another.

Himalayan salt lamps: Yes, salt is a crystal, and Himalayan salt lamps are excellent for clearing energy and purifying the air in a space. You can use either the electric or candle versions. Again, you'll need to use your sensory awareness to help you determine how many you need, what size, and where to put them.

When I first began my professional healing practice, I worked out of my studio apartment on the Upper East Side. Because I didn't want to be sleeping in my clients' energy every night, I became fastidious about space clearing. That paid off when I began renting therapy rooms by the hour at a healing and workshop center in Midtown. There were all kinds of practitioners working out of there, from massage therapists to life coaches to shamans to multidimensional psi doctors to psychics, and very few of them ever cleared the space. The energy would be so dense and heavy there sometimes that I would feel like I was walking through a thick fog when I entered the building. I was grateful to the center because the owners were nice and were making affordable space available to healers, but there came a point where it was too much to cope with and I started looking for someplace else.

Crystals to Help Shield or Hold Your Space

Some healers like to take the added step of placing crystals in their healing space to help shield and maintain the energy of the space at high, clear frequency. In order for crystal energy to effectively shield your space, the crystals have to be large enough to emit sufficient energy to be able to fill and surround your space. There's no general rule of thumb I can give in terms of size/energy/space ratio, but if the average crystal's aura is roughly ten times its size in diameter, in theory, you can roughly gauge how large or how many crystals you would need to shield a particular space. There are ways around this, however: Certain crystal shapes and combinations can work synergistically to increase the area of coverage. Pyramid and tower formations of crystals will amplify and direct their frequencies. You can also work with clear quartz clusters, points, and tabular formations, which will amplify and direct the frequencies of other crystals. Refer to the Tables of Correspondences starting on page 185 for a listing of crystals with protective and shielding properties.

Crystal-Shielding Suggestions

Please note that as every room's size and shape will be different, you will need to use your sensory awareness to gauge the appropriate size, number, and placement of your crystals. Consider the following strategies:

Amplifying protective energy: Place one or more protective crystals either on a large quartz cluster in the center of your room or on smaller clusters in all four corners. The quartz cluster will significantly amplify and magnify the crystals' energy, filling and surrounding the space.

Protective crystal grid: Place one quartz tower in the center of the room, surround the tower with black tourmaline crystals, and then surround the black tourmaline crystals with quartz points pointing outward, away from the black tourmalines, in a circular formation. Additionally, you can place either quartz or black tourmaline towers or pyramids in all four corners.

Pyramid and tower formations: Place protective crystals that have been shaped into pyramid or tower formations in all four corners and the center of your room. You can add a copper pyramid, hanging from the center of the ceiling, base down, to help unify and conduct the crystal energy in the space.

Salt perimeter:
Definitely the cheapest and simplest option, creating salt perimeters or sacred circles has been used for centuries to keep out dark energies and spirits. You can create a ring of sea salt around your healing space within the room or line the perimeter of the room with sea salt.

Step 4

PREPARING YOURSELF

As a healer, you are your business. If you're not capable of giving a healing session at a particular time, it doesn't matter how great your crystals are or how pure the reiki energy is, or even how lovely your healing space is. When giving a session, you need to be 100 percent committed to being of service.

This means your attention is focused on your client, his needs, and how best you can support him. If your mind's wandering; if you're feeling emotionally upset, stressed, or anxious; if you're physically ill; or if you're fantasizing or mentally writing your to-do list, you can't be 100 percent of service. This also holds true if you are judging your client, feel rushed or hungry, need to use the bathroom, or are physically uncomfortable in your space. The mind gets in the way and your needs or feelings will continue to pull at you instead of allowing you to stay focused.

Another consideration is your energy:
How strong is it? Even now, as you sit here reading this, are you grounded? Is your aura clear? Do you feel like your vibe is positive or negative? Do you feel in touch with Spirit? As a healer, you need to be grounded, with strong and clear energy, and a positive vibe from pre- to post-session. If you're lacking in any of these areas, it can detract from how well you're able to channel healing energy, receive intuitive guidance, remain present, and reduce the risk of any psychic attack or negative energy transference occurring during the session.

Your mind and your energy are the primary tools in your kit, and you need to take steps to make sure they're primed and ready to go.

Centering Meditation

For you to do any preparatory work effectively, you first must be able to do it with attention and intention. This means your mind must be your ally. In the contemporary world, our mind and attention are constantly being pulled in multiple directions simultaneously. Electronic devices, video screens, advertisements, social media, signs, messages, reading material, noise, light sources, thoughts, images, conversations—all go fleeting past us on a daily basis, constantly pulling at our attention. How do you tune this out? How can you quiet the mind, and let it all go, so you can focus and be 100 percent of service?

I have found that the single-most effective means by which we can achieve this is meditation, and while there are many forms and practices of meditation now, I recommend either a mindfulness style or what I call a centering meditation style.

With a centering meditation, I use my breath to drop my awareness down into what I call my center—the inner self, consciousness, or soul—to help me tune out the thoughts going on in my mind, any outside distractions, and my ego. Once I'm in that place, I find I'm far more tuned in to my intuition, psychic sensory abilities, and divine guidance. I also find that, once I'm in a meditative state, it's much easier for me to be in a place of wisdom and feel loving acceptance and compassion toward my clients. In healing, it's essential for us to be able to become quiet and drop into a place of inner stillness so that we may focus on what's in front of us, and be receptive to our inner, intuitive voice, as well as the pull of reiki energy, and the vibe we're feeling from our client and the crystals. For those of us who work with spirit guidance, this also helps us tune into the voice of the Divine. Maintaining a regular centering or mindfulness meditation practice helps us to cultivate that inner silence and soul-level engagement with what's happening in front of us.

It's most helpful to keep up a regular meditation practice of anywhere from 5 to 30 minutes daily, but you can also meditate from 5 to 30 minutes prior to your first healing session of the day.

Here's how to do a centering style meditation:

1. Find a quiet and comfortable place to sit where you won't be disturbed, set your timer, and close your eyes.

2. Begin by bringing awareness to your breathing, and just observe its quality: Is it shallow, deep, fast, gentle, labored, or easy? Give yourself this moment to fully tune into your breathing without judgment.

3. Now gently begin to deepen your breathing, imagining that you're breathing all the way down into what you feel is your center, wherever that might be to you. For some of us it's our heart, the core of our being, our womb, or somewhere in between. As you breathe into that place, allow your awareness to be gently guided there, and then settle into it.

4. If at any time you feel pulled back up to your thoughts or outside distractions, just brush them away and bring your awareness back to the breath, breathing down into your center.

5. Allow yourself to relax into that space, feeling the serenity and peace there as you do. Notice that while you are still aware of what's outside and around you, a buffer zone of calm and positive energy envelopes you.

6. In this space, you can open up to your intuition and your soul's voice by asking a question. Let the question be about something that can be of service or support to you, and then remain open and allow the answer to float up from that place (as opposed to trying to conjure it in your mind). Observe the answer "as is," without seeking to adjust, censor, or judge it.

7. The more you engage in this practice, the more easily you'll be able to drop into this space to hear your true, inner voice, and the guidance of your intuitive soul.

By practicing this meditation before doing a healing session, you'll have adjusted both your mind-set and your energy so you're in a place of receptivity and intuition, and focused on being of service to the work and your client. You can refer to the Tables of Correspondences starting on page 185 for a listing of crystals that can help you maintain a soul-centered focus.

Grounding

There are people who seem to think that to be a spiritual healer, you need to be considered above or superior to the material world. What you say, how you act, what you do, what you eat (or don't), the words you use, all have to be a reflection of some ideal or stereotype—the guru, the saint, the flighty hippie. The more detached and above it all you are, the more holy and reverent.

It may feel good on some surface level, but deep down it's rarely genuine. It's a mask, and ultimately people can sense it about you. If you're going to be doing healing work in the real world, with real people, you need to be real.

One of the compliments I've repeatedly received throughout my career has been "You're so *grounded*." Early on, I, too, felt that I had to be a certain way, talk a certain way, and come across a certain way to be respected and accepted as a healer. But as I got deeper into the work, I got over that. There's nothing more humbling than staring into someone's eyes as she's slowly dying, and listening to her ask for spiritual healing. In moments like those, it doesn't matter if you're a saint, a guru, a pure innocent being of light, or a boho hippie-chic wise woman. All that matters is whether you can compassionately hold space for that person and be of service. And if you're grounded and present, you can.

To be grounded means to be centered in your body, present, and aware of what's going on inside and around you. You're connected with your breathing, which is even and steady. You can feel your feet. You can respond, rather than react, to whatever's happening in the moment. You can experience your emotions while remaining in control of them, and you're able to focus on what you're doing whether mono- or multitasking. You're able to manage daily life and its obligations well, and can strike a healthy balance between your spiritual life and experiences, and those of your physical or material reality.

Being grounded is essential when you're a healer, because, frankly, there's a lot to do: You have to be present to your client and hear what he's saying to you, be able to respond to whatever he needs with compassion and wisdom, hold your ground if the need arises, select the appropriate crystals to work with, clear their aura, channel reiki effectively, stay focused during the session, tie up all loose ends, make recommendations, and then charge his credit card while scheduling his next appointment. That's the business of being a healer, and if your head or energy is somewhere else, how well are you going to handle all that?

Stereotypes aside, our modern lives conspire to unground us. Stress, anxiety, worry, overthinking, overworking, not sleeping enough, not having a healthy diet or lifestyle, having too much to do/manage/organize, and the nervous emotional energy that entails can all unground us. Resistance to feeling or experiencing emotions, which then leads us to breathe shallowly and get caught up in our thoughts, is also a major contributor to feeling ungrounded.

That's life, and life happens all the time, so here are a few ways you can help ground yourself before a session:

> **Go for a short walk** and feel your feet connect with the ground with each step.

> **Sit on the floor** (or preferably under a tree), and feel your energy sink into the ground below you, or imagine growing roots from your root chakra all the way down to the center of the Earth.

> **Eat food that takes a long time to digest**, like fibrous root and cruciferous vegetables, whole grains, and sources of either plant-or animal-based protein.

> **Pay attention to your breathing.** If it's rapid and/or shallow, mindfully slow it down and deepen it into your body for at least a full minute.

> **Use the centering meditation** technique (page 97) to guide your consciousness out of your mind and back into your body.

> **Engage in some form of vigorous exercise**, like dancing, jumping rope, jogging, or martial arts to get yourself back in your body.

You can refer to the Tables of Correspondences starting on page 185 for a listing of crystals that you can wear or meditate with to promote grounding as well.

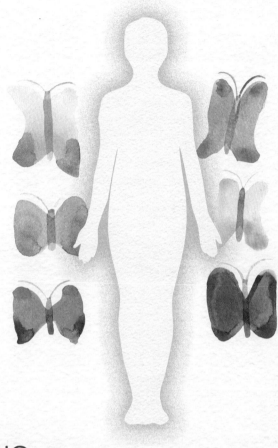

STEP 5

PREPARING YOUR CLIENT

So your crystals are ready, your room is set up and cleared, and your energy is grounded, centered, purified, and shielded. Now it's time for you to meet your client. From the time your client enters to when she leaves the room, she is your priority and being of service should be your sole focus. Hence the importance of doing all your prep work first! Find out why she's there, what she's seeking to address, and how she's hoping to be supported.

Support is a key word here: You're not working miracles, offering cures, diagnosing issues and divining solutions, or solving her problems. Make sure she knows what to expect from the session, and that her expectations are realistic.

You're there to offer support by helping to provide the energy she needs to heal and help herself. I've had plenty of clients come in expecting me to "wave a magic wand" or give them answers that their therapists, doctors, or health care practitioners haven't been able to provide. That's not my job, and it's not yours. Establishing boundaries and maintaining transparency are very important; otherwise, you can get yourself into trouble.

I was once so invested in helping a bipolar client experience an emotional connection in her acting work that I overstepped that boundary. I felt determined to help her break through, and I remember one day saying words of encouragement that prompted her to snap back at me, asking me, "Well, when are you going to make this happen?!" Whoa. That's when I stepped back and realized that I had gone out of bounds with my work. Because I had tried to go the extra mile to help her and had felt a conviction that the energy work could solve her problem, she had projected the responsibility of her progress and process onto me. This is where the reiki teaching of not allowing yourself to become attached to result is so valuable.

As a healer, it is not you bringing about results, it is the energy and your client's willingness, ability, and desire to heal that are responsible for the healing process. Your sole responsibility is to help create the environment and provide the energy support you feel your client needs while he is in a session with you. That's it, and it's very important for your client to understand this right up front. Healers can fall prey to accusations of misrepresentation, fraudulence, or charlatanism when this boundary isn't honored.

Asking a client what energy or support she needs helps to empower her in her own process. It's not about what you can do for her, it's about what she needs to do for herself. We tend to project a lot of our own power and authority onto others. When a client realizes that it's within her own power to help, transform, or heal herself, the healing has already begun, and you're free to do your work with integrity and without the impediments of unrealistic demands or expectations.

Consulting with your client also provides the valuable opportunity to start getting a feel for which crystals he may need in the session. Pay attention to what he's saying, but also the vibe you're feeling from him and any intuitive guidance that may come through. Consider the issues he's facing—which chakras do they relate to? Where are you getting a feeling that they might be blocked or need a boost? Which emotions is he powerfully expressing, or do you sense he may be holding back? All of these are valuable questions to contemplate during or after your consultation.

Once you've completed your consultation, and you have ideas in mind in terms of crystals and reiki hand placements, your client can hop on your table and you can begin your practice.

Part 3

THE PRACTICE

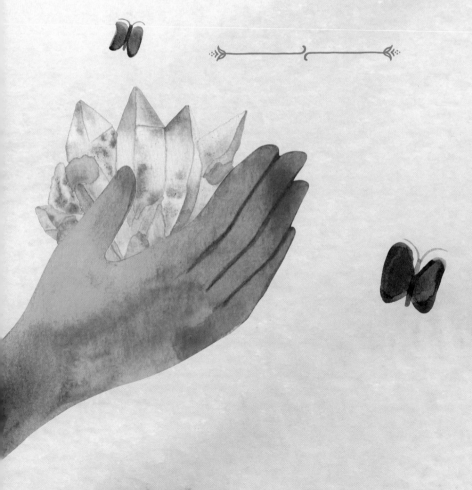

HEALING SESSION

Now that you've done all your prep work, it's time for the healing session! In Part 3 I'm offering what I consider to be "crystal gold": crystal combinations and layouts (which I refer to as "protocols"), culled from over thirteen years of client session notes and personal experience, that you can use in your Crystal Reiki sessions to help effect healing. It's formatted in such a way that you can use it as a handy reference guide in your sessions, but also read through the case studies and anecdotes for examples of how the protocols can be applied for physical, emotional, mental, spiritual, and aura healing. While there are thousands of crystals I could reference, I've distilled them all down to make suggestions based on what most consistently worked and proved successful for my clients in addressing symptoms as well as underlying causes.

SYMPTOMS VERSUS UNDERLYING CAUSES

Where Crystal Reiki goes deep and can become very powerful is when it's being applied to address not just symptoms, but also their underlying causes. You can put a bandage on a cut, but if the glass is still in the wound, you'll need to go deeper with the treatment or the wound will only fester. This holds true for all levels of healing, whether physical, emotional, mental, or spiritual. If your work addresses only the symptoms, you'll help people feel more comfortable, but you won't necessarily be helping them heal. I've seen this time and again in my healing practice—clients seeking help with their stress, anxiety, pain, upset, mental blocks, or trauma, and often expecting the crystals and reiki to just whisk it away. Hey, I can sympathize! As a human being, when I'm suffering, I want the suffering to stop. But, as a healer, I know that the only path to true balance and wellness is addressing what's *causing the imbalance and suffering in the first place.*

You can determine underlying causes by asking open-ended questions, like "Do you know the source of your stress?" or "What do you feel, deep down, you're getting out of this situation?" and listening to what your client has to say. Trust your gut, and always err on the side of compassion and being a good listener. Sometimes your client may know the cause, sometimes she may have to think about it. If you have an intuition about a cause, you can suggest it but, again, do this in the form of a question: "Do you have a fear of being alone if you leave your husband?" and, if so, "Where do you think that comes from?" Telling your client what you think is wrong with her is a big no-no.

It's disempowering, and it denies her the opportunity to come to her own healing realization, which can have a much more profound effect on her psyche. It might also create a sense of distrust in her if she thinks you're wrong, or it might even potentially lead to conflict if you trigger her.

What if you can't determine the underlying cause? Then you address the symptoms in hopes that the cause(s) will come to light in time. Sometimes, when the discomfort of the symptoms has been diminished, it's easier for your client to identify their underlying cause. I remember when a client of mine, a struggling actress, was frustrated by her lack of motivation and her tendency to sabotage good opportunities when they came her way. She couldn't figure out why she kept showing up late to agent interviews, blowing auditions, and turning down roles because she didn't find them appealing. I suggested she let it go for now and give herself permission to just relax and receive, and I used protocols for ambition, self-love, and stress relief during the session to help her feel more motivated, to forgive herself, and to reduce the feelings of frustration that might be blocking her from grasping the source of her self-sabotage. At the end of the session, she sat up and said, "Oh my God. I think I know why I'm sabotaging myself!" A memory had surfaced of a time when, at the age of five, she had told her mother that she was going to be an actress, and her mother had replied that she'd never make it: She'd be a receptionist or an assistant or a maid, like the rest of the women in her family. My client sat there and sobbed for 10 minutes, and then felt twenty pounds lighter. The energy she had received during the session had helped her to relax and let go deeply enough that she was able to access the information she needed in her subconscious. It had also given her some of the feelings of self-love and motivation she needed to see that she *could* achieve her dreams. A month later she was in LA meeting with movie producers, and her career was finally getting on track.

Obviously, your clients won't always experience dramatic results from a single Crystal Reiki session, but it definitely can happen. Healing is a process that takes time. If you're working steadfastly toward addressing underlying causes, as well as their symptoms, I do believe that healing is inevitable. The important thing to note is that, as a Crystal Reiki healer, your job is to provide the healing energy your clients need to heal themselves, and that's it: The rest is on them. If your clients are on board with the process and are making choices and taking actions toward their healing goal, then my experience has been that they'll likely achieve it. However, if they're resisting or in denial, or are refusing to make changes in support of their healing goals, unfortunately the Crystal Reiki energy probably won't be enough.

I had a client who was suffering from leaky gut syndrome (a condition of intestinal permeability due to damage caused to the small intestine, which allows food particles and bacteria to leak into the bloodstream), likely caused by a gluten intolerance. She was also working a day job that she hated while she was writing her PhD thesis. She was Italian, so despite her awareness that she had a gluten intolerance, she would turn to her favorite starchy comfort foods when she came home at night. She wouldn't leave the day job because she said she needed the money, and she wouldn't cut out the bread and pasta, but she was hoping I could still work wonders with Crystal Reiki. I explained to her that I could help ease her symptoms, but unless she was willing to make changes in her lifestyle, I couldn't effectively support her in her process of healing and recovery. She came to see me for a few sessions and always felt better afterward, but she eventually gave up because she wasn't seeing any significant results beyond that. The sad truth is that no matter which healer she goes to see or what new modality she tries, as long as she persists in her unhealthy choices, she's not going to get better.

I make it a practice to never judge my clients. We're *all* in our own healing process, and some things are easier for us to face while others need more time and experience. None of us come out of the womb perfect, and very few of us leave the Earth that way, either. Crystal Reiki isn't a magic cure-all; it's something that can provide the energy someone needs for his healing process. If, like with my client, your client isn't fully willing to engage in that process, take responsibility for his choices and actions, and make the necessary changes, he's wasting his money because he'll be working against the energy he's receiving in his healing sessions. If he starts to turn his frustration or project his disappointments onto you, it's time to consider lovingly but firmly severing ties with that client, or refusing to work with him until he's willing to change. This can be a difficult move to make, especially if you care about your client, but you can't take responsibility for his choices or accountability for his improvement. All you can do is provide the energy and the healing environment that supports him. The rest is up to him.

SELECTING YOUR PROTOCOLS

Once you've determined what your client wants to address, both in terms of symptoms and (hopefully) causes, it's time to choose your crystals. This can be the most complicated, but also most fun, part of your practice. You can make selections based on what you feel most needs to be addressed in the session. While I've emphasized the importance of working on resolving underlying causes, it is crucial to also help your client address her symptoms. This will help her to feel more comfortable and relaxed during the session, which in turns allows the crystal and reiki energy to flow more freely, potentially activating deeper levels of healing.

ATTUNING TO NEW CRYSTALS

Whether you choose to work with the protocols in this book, or follow those based on your own experience and intuition with crystals, it's very important for you to work only with crystals with which you're familiar. I always train my students to attune to a crystal and read about it first before working with it in healing, either for themselves or others. Attuning to a crystal means familiarizing yourself with its energy and its impact on your system. The simplest way to do this is to read about it in a crystal reference book and then hold it in your receptive hand. Meditate on it with your awareness for 5 to 10 minutes, making note of how it makes you feel or what kind of effect it has on you. Because crystals are your energy tools and allies in Crystal Reiki, it's simply a matter of being professional to know what you're working with before you use it in healing.

SUBSTITUTIONS

What happens if you don't have one of the crystals suggested in a given protocol? You've got options: You can dash out and buy it, choose a different protocol to use, or make a substitution. As I mentioned previously, I'm giving specific crystal recommendations based on my own successful experience, but that doesn't exclude the possibility of other crystals working effectively as alternatives. For instance, if a protocol calls for the use of morganite for compassion but you don't have any morganite, you could substitute rose quartz or chrysocolla instead.

The important thing is to know the properties of your crystals and how they function. You don't want to sub in a crystal that has properties that will counteract the desired effect of a protocol or undermine your client's energy needs. For instance, selenite helps to relieve stress but it's also ungrounding, so it wouldn't be a smart substitute in a stress relief protocol for someone who's also struggling to remain grounded. Carnelian is great for empowerment, but when placed on an excessive sacral chakra, it could cause that chakra to become even more excessive.

Allow your crystal wisdom and your intuition to guide you in your choices when it comes to substitutions. There may also be times when you have all the crystals you need, and you've chosen your protocols, and yet your gut keeps guiding you to try something else. Ultimately, trust your gut, because our crystals speak to us through our intuition. If you've done your prep work properly, as outlined in Part 2, you'll be tuned in to your client's energy and your Crystal Reiki vibes, and your intuition may have picked up on something that your conscious mind has missed. As long as you know what you're working with and your intention is for your client's highest healing good, you'll likely choose the best crystal for him 99.9 percent of the time.

CRYSTAL REIKI FOR PHYSICAL HEALING

People are often pleasantly surprised the first time they experience the healing effects of crystals on the physical body. That crystals might affect us psychically or emotionally is a little easier for people to accept, but when pain is significantly reduced or healing is noticeably accelerated, that can shock the heck out of some! I recently had a crystal healing student report to me that she used some of the protocols below on a reiki client of hers who was suffering from tendonitis, and he called her the next day to say that his pain had been reduced by 75 percent. He couldn't believe it! And then he booked another session.

In my years of doing this work with clients, I've applied crystal healing techniques to address broken bones, bruises, burns, digestive issues, fibroids, fertility issues, heart and lung illnesses, as well as the common cold and various autoimmune diseases. Given that New York City is such a smorgasboard of people and problems, I had the opportunity to work on a multitude of challenges during my years of professional healing work. I noted a particularly high success rate with the effects of Crystal Reiki healing on tissue and bone repair, digestive disorders, chronic pain, muscular tension, inflammation, and the acceleration of recovery from injury and illness.

Let's be clear that in no way was I "playing doctor." I was a spiritual healer, and I made no claims to diagnose, treat, or cure anything physical.

I'd always encourage clients to seek out medical advice and treatment, and I'd never counsel going against medical advice or treatment. I'd make it clear that my role was to help provide whatever supplemental energy may be of service to a person and his healing process, even if it was just helping him to cope with the stress of it. This is important to note, because if you're not aware of this and take your work or claims too far, it could land you in a lot of legal hot water, depending on the laws governing where you live and practice. I never refused someone who was seeking help with a physical ailment, provided he understood and accepted what I could provide by means of support, and what I could not.

As I write this, there are still a lot of modern ailments and illnesses that are difficult to understand, diagnose, or treat in the world of modern medicine. I am not critical of modern medicine; it saves countless lives every single day. But in a world of growing stress, anxiety, fear, limited access to mental and physical health care, and a list of disorders that are still very much in a gray area, it's important for us healers to know that more and more people with physical health and healing needs are going to be showing up on our doorsteps. And we need to know how to deal with them appropriately.

Be sure to be well-versed in the laws governing where you live and honor them, and then provide whatever healing support you can with integrity. Beware of clients who come to see you and ask you to confirm, negate, or provide a medical diagnosis. Unless you're a trained medical intuitive, a licensed health care practitioner, or a doctor, that is not your job. Also, be cautious with clients who want help with a medical condition but are vague or unclear as to how they think you can help them or what results they're seeking from the work. Perhaps all you can do is support them in managing the stress of their condition. Sometimes even being willing to just listen and care can be a deeply healing experience for clients. Always work from the heart, be honest, be willing to listen, and offer your best.

PHYSICAL HEALING PROTOCOLS

Place the following crystals as described. Use reiki hand placements and symbols as you feel guided, or as indicated. All crystals are to be placed over the area of illness or injury, except where chakras are specified. You can check out the Crystal Index starting on page 192 to determine their healing or metaphysical properties.

In cases of serious disease, remember that the crystal energy is offering support to the body's natural healing process, not providing a treatment or cure.

A note on crystal placements at the root chakra: Because the root chakra falls somewhere between the genitals and the base of the spine, a rather "sensitive" area of the body, most people will find it inappropriate for you to be placing crystals there. You can cheat the root chakra crystal placements by putting them on the body a couple of inches above the genital area near the belt line or by placing them at the top of either thigh where it meets the hip joint.

Accelerating the body's healing or recovery process: Celestite, hematite, malachite, bloodstone, or red jasper have all demonstrated an ability to accelerate the body's natural healing and recovery process.

Adrenal fatigue or deficiency: Place a piece of chrysocolla and ocean jasper over the area of each adrenal gland to help restore balance, and citrine on the solar plexus chakra to help replenish the level of chi.

Arthritis: Celestite helps reduce inflammation, hematite helps fortify the joint, and selenite is useful in managing pain. Place all three on the arthritic part of the body.

Asthma: Place blue jade, selenite, and emerald on the upper part of the chest to help relieve a feeling of tightness and congestion, and to increase the healing flow of chi through the area. Use a counterclockwise cho ku rei to help relieve congestion and remove blocked energy.

Autoimmune diseases:
Autoimmune disease is an umbrella term that encompasses many illnesses in which the body's immune system attacks its own organs. To help address an autoimmune disease with Crystal Reiki, use the immune support protocol, the inflammation protocol, and then apply reiki to whichever organ(s) is affected.

Brain injuries: Selenite, fluorite, healer's gold, and sugilite, either placed at the crown chakra or over the third eye chakra, can support the body in reducing pain and inflammation, improving overall function, and repairing damaged tissue.

Bronchitis: Selenite, green tourmaline, celestite, and green calcite placed on the upper chest help to relieve congestion, reduce coughing, and create a greater feeling of spaciousness in the area. Use only hovering reiki hand positions over the chest to avoid adding any sensations of physical pressure.

Bruises: Place black tourmaline and selenite on the area of the bruise to help slow the blood flow, accelerate the healing of capillaries and blood vessels, and reduce pain and swelling.

Burns: Never place crystals on a burn unless it has already been cleaned, bandaged, and received medical attention. Place celestite to soothe and cool the burn; and malachite, red jasper, and bloodstone to accelerate the healing and regeneration of tissue. If the burn area is too painful, avoid the placement of crystals and channel hands-off reiki into the area. If it is a second- or third-degree burn, draw the Tibetan dai ko myo and hover your hands lightly over the area.

Cancer: Place the following crystals over the affected area(s) to help support the body's fight against the cancer cells: smoky elestial quartz, unakite, green tourmaline, sugilite, epidote, and charoite. Never place clear quartz on a client who has cancer, because you run the risk that the quartz energy could accelerate cancerous growths.

COPD (chronic obstructive pulmonary disease): Place selenite for the congestion, emerald to help improve air flow, malachite to increase healthy flow of chi, and azurite to help ease tension in the lung area. For women, you will need to place these crystals on the heart chakra area just above the breasts, or in between the breasts if they are comfortable with that placement. Always honor personal boundaries before proceeding.

Crohn's disease: This chronic inflammatory disease is challenging to address because it can affect any part of the gastrointestinal tract, from the mouth to the rectum, but most commonly it targets the small intestine and the colon. You'll need to consult with your client in terms of where he most often feels symptoms, and localize your crystal placements as best you can in that general area. You can use black tourmaline to help neutralize causes of imbalance, celestite or aquamarine to help soothe and reduce inflammation, and bloodstone or hematite to help improve overall wellness in the area.

Detox (physical): Galena at both feet will help to draw out toxins, and placing red calcite at the root chakra will help support an overall detox from the body, while charoite over the liver or gold rutilated quartz over the kidneys will help to purge toxins from those organs.

Digestion, inflammation: Place celestite and aquamarine over the area to reduce inflammation and soothe tissue, and tiger's eye and honey calcite on the abdominal area to help support healthy digestion.

Digestion, poor or sluggish: Place citrine, tiger iron, and copper on the solar plexus chakra to help build and sustain digestive fire and energy.

You can also draw a clockwise cho ku rei to send healing energy and strength into the area.

Energy, boosting vitality: Put a shiva lingam in both hands, and a Boji stone at each foot, to send vitality, strength, and energy into your client's body. You can also place ruby and red jasper on the root chakra to increase vitality and flow of chi.

Fertility: Place carnelian, a shiva lingam, ruby, copper, and healer's gold over the womb area to increase flow of chi and fertile energy. You can also draw a Tibetan dai ko myo and a clockwise cho ku rei over the womb area if your client is struggling to conceive, or send a counterclockwise cho ku rei into the right or left fallopian tube if there is a blockage.

Fibroids: Put celestite, malachite, and bloodstone over the area of the inflamed fibroid to help reduce swelling, inflammation, and discomfort. You can also place orange calcite on the sacral chakra to increase the flow of healing chi to the area, and black tourmaline to stop or slow the growth.

Fibromyalgia: Place a selenite stick or smaller pieces of selenite along the spinal cord to help deliver pain relief throughout the nervous system.

Headache, migraine: Place celestite as close to the epicenter of the pain as possible without actually touching the head. For sinus and eye strain–related headaches, place azurite on the forehead. Avoid placing quartz or selenite anywhere near the head, as this can exacerbate the pain.

Heart disease: There are a range of conditions that can affect the heart, including blockages or narrowing of the arteries and blood vessels, as well as rhythm issues and defects. Overall healing crystals for the physical heart are green tourmaline, red tourmaline, malachite, sugilite, and healer's gold. Place as many as you can fit over the physical heart for male clients, or on the heart chakra for female clients, to help infuse the area with healing and fortifying energy.

High blood pressure: See the "Stress Relief" protocols listed in "Mental and Emotional Healing," page 122.

HIV (human immunodeficiency virus): Apply immune-boosting and energy-boosting protocols with the addition of smoky elestial quartz held in your client's receptive hand for increased healing light in the body, and reiki hand placements over the root, solar plexus, and heart chakras, and cradling under the head to send healing energy into the major glands of the endocrine system (which supports a healthy immune system).

Immune system, support: Put ruby, red calcite, and red jasper on the root chakra to help boost the body's overall immune system and vitality. Add citrine at the solar plexus to strengthen the gut flora, and green aventurine at the heart chakra to increase cardiovascular health and support.

Impotence, virility: Place red jasper and pyrite at the root chakra to increase testosterone, shiva lingam in both hands for potency and strength, and fire agate at the sacral chakra to boost libido.

Inflammation, general: Place either selenite, celestite, or aquamarine over the affected area to help reduce inflammation.

Insomnia, jet lag: If your client is suffering from sleeplessness, disrupted sleep patterns, or is recovering from jet lag, place mookaite jasper and apache tear at the root for grounding, stabilizing, and settling back into her body's natural rhythm; lepidolite at the crown to help reset healthy sleep patterns; and amethyst on the third eye chakra to reduce any stress or anxiety contributing to the problem.

Irritable bowel syndrome (IBS): On the lower abdomen, place celestite and aquamarine to reduce inflammation, and tiger's eye and honey calcite or dravite for resiliency, ease, and to support overall healthy bowel function.

Lower back pain: Place a minimum of two pieces of selenite to reduce pain, along with black tourmaline to help minimize the formation of any energy blockage, and malachite to help accelerate recovery. Place one hand on the lower back, the other on the top of the hamstrings, to channel extra reiki to the area.

Muscle soreness: Place or tape hematite, red jasper, and bloodstone to help ease muscle pain and accelerate the healing of tears or tissue repair. Selenite can be used for tension relief.

Ovarian cysts: Place small pieces of celestite, malachite, sugilite, green tourmaline, and bloodstone over the general area of the cyst to relieve inflammation, stop or slow growth, and reduce the size of the cyst.

Pain, general: You can place selenite on any area of the body that is in pain. I consider it second only to the effects of an ice pack, and it works faster than a pain pill.

Pregnancy: Crystal placements on the belly should be completely avoided, with one exception, for the full term, so as not to expose the unborn child to any potentially unbalancing crystal energy. If there is concern that the fetus is being affected by the mother's emotional stress, the exception to the rule is that you can safely place jet on the belly to help relieve the stress. Jet absorbs far more energy than it emits, so it can help to reduce the energy of stress in the womb area without significantly affecting the unborn child. Safe crystal placements for the lower body are red calcite or ruby at the root chakra for vitality, and honey calcite at the solar plexus for ease. From the heart chakra up, you can place whatever is needed to help support the mother in her mental, emotional, and spiritual healing process.

Premenstrual syndrome (PMS): Place selenite, malachite, red jasper, and aquamarine over the womb to help ease general symptoms, including cramping, bloating, discomfort, fatigue, and moodiness. Avoid placing hematite or bloodstone on the body if your client experiences heavy blood flow, as they may increase the flow.

Shoulder tension: Place or tape two pieces of selenite and rose quartz on the back of both shoulders to eliminate pain and tension, and to bring greater feelings of comfort to that part of the body.

Sore throat: Place blue kyanite and blue calcite on the throat to help relieve symptoms and accelerate recovery from illness.

Sprains: If there is sufficient room on the body, place malachite, selenite, and green tourmaline or green aventurine on the sprain. These crystals will help to manage symptoms of pain and swelling while dramatically accelerating the body's natural healing and recovery process. If there isn't sufficient space or if the sprain is at an awkward angle on the body, hold a piece of selenite in your hand over the area of injury and channel reiki through the selenite.

Tears, ligament/tendon/ cartilage: Put hematite, red jasper, and celestite or aquamarine over the afflicted area to increase blood flow, accelerate the healing and repair of tissue, and reduce any inflammation or swelling that could impede the healing flow of chi.

Weight loss: There's almost always a mental, emotional, and sometimes even a spiritual component to weight issues. I've noticed over the years (and from my own experience) that many healers tend to gain weight around the stomach and abdominal area as a means of insulating themselves from their clients' energy. Be sure to consult with your client first about what he feels may be the underlying causes, and then seek to address those as well. For physical weight issues, place blue apatite on the throat to reduce the urge to eat, green aventurine on the heart chakra to increase overall metabolic rate, citrine on the solar plexus to increase digestive energy and improve the processing of fats and carbohydrates, bloodstone on the sacral chakra to help balance any tendencies toward excess, and ruby and apache tear at the root to increase overall stamina and vitality during exercise.

Mental and Emotional Healing

Emotional healing, in particular, is my specialty. I had countless clients who came to see me saying that they were tired of just talking through their problems and feelings; they were ready to do something about them. The powerful thing about crystals is that their energy vibrations flow right into the subconscious, the emotional body, and the psyche, so that you're able to address issues directly with energy healing. The application of reiki helps to harmonize and support the flow of this work to help balance extremes, and to allow your client to remain relaxed and receptive during the session.

Stress Relief

Reducing stress should be on every Crystal Reiki practitioner's calling card. Clearing stress from the body is one of the easiest things to do with this combined modality, and the value of that should not be underestimated. It seems as if all of us, including (literally) our cat and dog, is experiencing stress; it's reached epic proportions in our society. Stress manifests on every level, and works its way down through every subtle field of our being: spiritual, mental, emotional, and then physical. By the time it reaches the physical, it starts to make us sick, and if we're already sick, it exacerbates our symptoms and illness. Stress will also slow or block the healing and recovery process. For these reasons it's become essential to clear stress out of the body to support health and wellness. That being said, it's also very important to address the underlying causes of the stress, if you can, to help improve your client's overall wellness.

CASE STUDY:
Madeleine

Madeleine's source of stress was that she was afraid of losing her job. She had a high-powered position at an international organization, and she was just a couple years shy of retirement. There were major turnovers and overhauls happening in several departments, including hers, and a lot of the new hires were young and inexperienced workers who were willing to accept lower salaries. In order to prove the worth of her talent and experience, Madeleine was putting in extra-long work hours, often without taking a break even to eat, and was triple-checking everything to avoid any potential inaccuracies or problems. She'd go into meetings and would be so stressed, so anxious, and so unsure of herself, that she found it almost impossible to articulate her thoughts well, promote her ideas, or assert her authority and honor her boundaries.

One of Madeleine's colleagues, sensing her insecurity, became ruthless in pointing out wherever Madeleine made mistakes, interrupting or talking over her at meetings, and making snide comments about Madeleine being unable to keep up with the workload. While this infuriated her, she was too afraid to say anything, lest she rock the boat further. She was miserable, and her guts would twist so badly every Sunday night at the thought of returning to work on Monday, that she would barely sleep the whole night.

When Madeleine would arrive for her sessions with me, her body would be stiff as a board, and you could feel the stress and anxiety vibrating off her in waves through her aura. At first she was just looking for relief, a way to cope with the ordeal of her situation and possibly find some respite. As we worked together week after week, I began to suggest ways that we could deepen the energy work and possibly help her more. Madeleine, bless her, was open to any and all things that might help her feel better and improve her situation, so we began to layer in some emotional and mental healing protocols, along with the stress relief work. Session by session, we worked with protocols for empowerment; freeing up her voice so she could articulate her thoughts and ideas clearly; gaining the courage to be seen and heard; cultivating self-love, self-worth, and nurturing, as well as intuition for greater insight and foresight while she was at work.

Here's an example of a Crystal Reiki layout I would place on Madeleine, incorporating the self-worth, communication, and boundary protocols that are described in the following pages.

Root: Ruby

Sacral: Carnelian

Solar Plexus: Sunstone and Tiger's Eye

Heart: Rhodochrosite, Rose Quartz, Rhodonite, Green Aventurine

Throat: Aquamarine

Third Eye: Amethyst

Crown: Moonstone

Feet: Smoky Quartz

CRYSTAL KEY

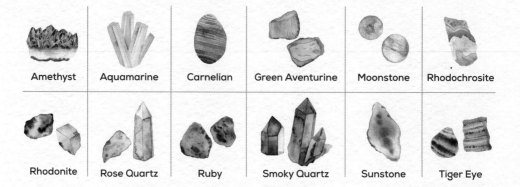

Amethyst	Aquamarine	Carnelian	Green Aventurine	Moonstone	Rhodochrosite
Rhodonite	Rose Quartz	Ruby	Smoky Quartz	Sunstone	Tiger Eye

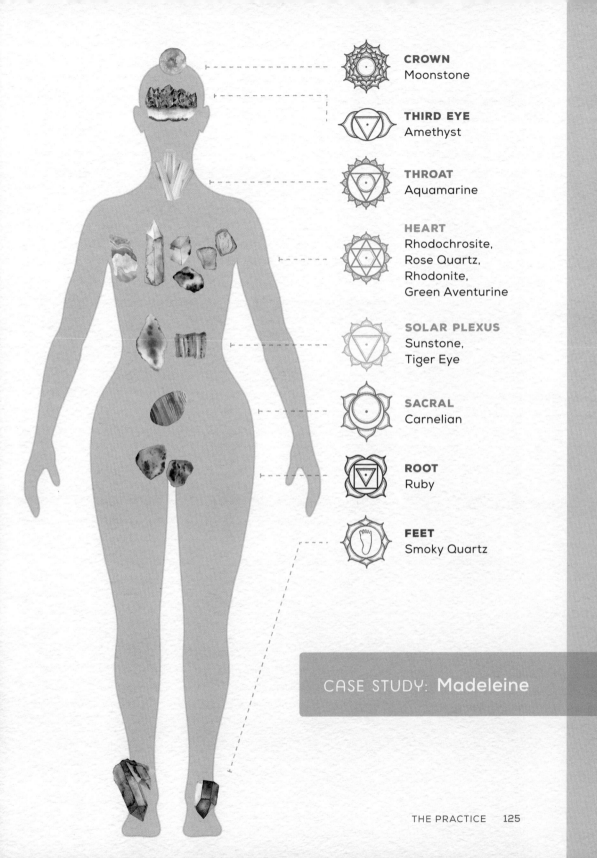

CROWN
Moonstone

THIRD EYE
Amethyst

THROAT
Aquamarine

HEART
Rhodochrosite,
Rose Quartz,
Rhodonite,
Green Aventurine

SOLAR PLEXUS
Sunstone,
Tiger Eye

SACRAL
Carnelian

ROOT
Ruby

FEET
Smoky Quartz

CASE STUDY: **Madeleine**

While many heads rolled at her organization, Madeleine's was not one of them. Slowly but surely, step by step, she began to stand more in her power. She still put in long hours, but she spoke up at meetings, supported her own ideas, delegated more, boosted morale among her new workers, and stood up to her bullying colleague (who was eventually transferred). She was still grappling with the lingering fear of losing her job, but she developed a growing confidence that if she did, she would do so on her own terms with her head held high. Happily, Madeleine made it through those last two years with a growing sense of self, and higher hopes and expectations for the next phase of her life to be enjoyed in retirement.

Emotional Wounds

While stress may be a common, even uniting factor among your clients, everything else will run the gamut when it comes to mental and emotional healing with Crystal Reiki. Heartache, heartbreak, grief and loss, anger, anxiety, trauma, recovery, insecurity, low self-worth, loneliness, feeling stuck or lost, turbulent transitions, childhood abuse, self-abuse—I've pretty much seen it all in my practice. Your client's mental and emotional needs will likely be complicated, involving any number of issues or challenges, and it's important to remember that emotional healing takes time. "Time heals all," as they say, and while we can help support and accelerate the process with energy work, it can't be rushed or forced. The emotional body will always take the time it needs, so as healers we have to sometimes counsel both ourselves and our clients to have patience.

Johnny

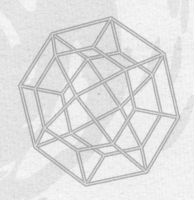

Johnny was a sweet and kind man who was in recovery from alcoholism. He had been a functional alcoholic for over a decade, and had been prone to angry and sometimes violent outbursts. In the year that led up to his choice to become sober, he had lost his job, his family, and his home to his addiction, and these losses prompted him to quit drinking and get sober. He was celebrating his first year of sobriety when he started working with me. He wanted to get his life back on track, find a good job, and reconcile with his wife and daughter. As the numbing effects of the alcohol wore off, he was feeling an enormous amount of anger, shame, regret, and pain, but also hope.

He wanted help coping with his emotions, he wanted to heal the hurts of the past, and he wanted to find ways to safely release the pent-up anger he was feeling inside. As we began working together, he also revealed that in therapy he had uncovered memories of having been sexually abused when he was a child. He suspected that this was the underlying cause of his drinking problem. He also wondered if, once he had healed and resolved his feelings, he could begin to drink again in moderation. His wife ran a successful group of wine bars and restaurants in the city, and drinking had always been part of their lifestyle.

I couldn't give him any answers, of course; it wasn't my place. But I did strongly encourage him to take it one step at a time. Johnny had over ten years' worth of emotional energy surfacing, and a lot of healing and other work to do in his life. Many people want to get clear of their anger right away, and jump to forgiveness, but it doesn't work that way. First, Johnny had to accept everything that had happened, which didn't mean he was condoning it all, just acknowledging and accepting that it had happened. Anger needs to be heard and acknowledged, because it always has a message. Whether a boundary has been crossed or violated, something else is wrong, or something's being ignored or denied, anger (as with all emotions) carries information. For years, so much inside Johnny had needed to be heard, but it was drowned out by alcohol instead.

Here's an example of a Crystal Reiki layout I would use for Johnny, incorporating the anger and childhood trauma protocols from the following pages:

Root: Apache Tear and Snowflake Obsidian

Sacral: Bloodstone

Solar Plexus: Honey Calcite and Rhodochrosite

Heart: Mangano Calcite, Sugilite, Malachite, and Pink Kunzite

Throat: Chrysocolla

Third Eye: Amethyst

Crown: Moonstone

Hands: Aragonite Star Cluster (receptive), Smoky Elestial Quartz (dominant)

Feet: Hematite

CRYSTAL KEY

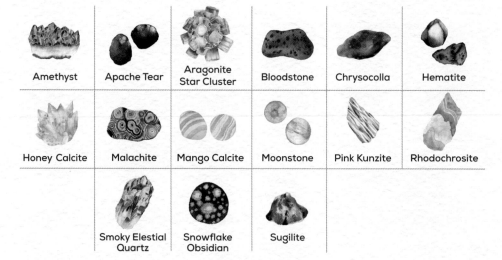

Amethyst	Apache Tear	Aragonite Star Cluster	Bloodstone	Chrysocolla	Hematite
Honey Calcite	Malachite	Mango Calcite	Moonstone	Pink Kunzite	Rhodochrosite
	Smoky Elestial Quartz	Snowflake Obsidian	Sugilite		

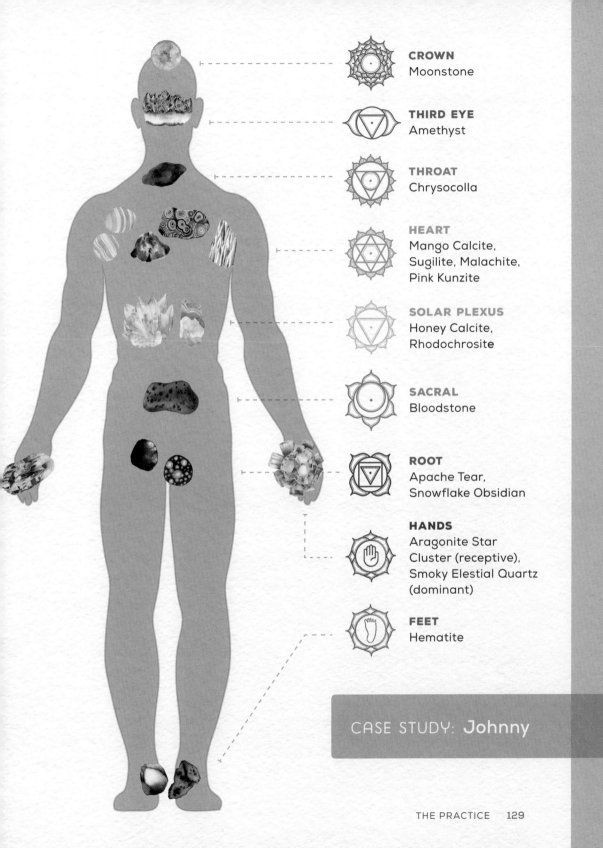

CROWN
Moonstone

THIRD EYE
Amethyst

THROAT
Chrysocolla

HEART
Mango Calcite,
Sugilite, Malachite,
Pink Kunzite

SOLAR PLEXUS
Honey Calcite,
Rhodochrosite

SACRAL
Bloodstone

ROOT
Apache Tear,
Snowflake Obsidian

HANDS
Aragonite Star
Cluster (receptive),
Smoky Elestial Quartz
(dominant)

FEET
Hematite

CASE STUDY: **Johnny**

Johnny didn't have an easy recovery, but he persisted with such an open heart and the willingness to communicate that in time his wife and daughter forgave him, and he was happily reunited with his family. Not only had his own process convinced him that healing and living a happy, sober life was possible, but it also sparked a passion in him to help others with their own healing and recovery process. Along with taking a few of my crystal healing workshops, he enrolled in college to pursue his MSW (master of social work) degree, so that he could one day provide counseling for alcohol and abuse victims.

CRYSTAL REIKI PROTOCOLS FOR MENTAL AND EMOTIONAL HEALING

Place the following crystals as described. Use reiki hand placements and symbols as you feel guided, or as indicated.

Abuse, healing or recovering from: Place rhodochrosite, mangano calcite, and watermelon tourmaline at the heart chakra for deep emotional healing of trauma; chrysoprase and citrine at the solar plexus for an increased sense of security and personal power; orange calcite and bloodstone at the sacral chakra for emotional strength, stability, and healing of the sacral chakra; and apache tear for healing of grief, loss, and fear at the root chakra.

Acceptance: Place mangano calcite on the heart chakra or in the receptive hand for gentle acceptance and healing energy; and tiger's eye or honey calcite on the solar plexus for an increased sense of security, confidence, and openness to change.

Addictions: Place unakite on the heart chakra, amethyst in the receptive hand, and hematite in the dominant hand to help support the releasing of harmful habits, emotional or chemical dependencies, and addictions; the shifting of negative thought patterns; and the gentle purging of emotional and chemical toxins. You can add black obsidian and snowflake obsidian at the root chakra or at the feet to help keep your clients grounded in their inner truth, healing process, and to support them in making choices that are more in alignment with their higher selves. Draw a Tibetan dai ko myo into all seven chakras.

Ambition: Place pyrite and citrine on the solar plexus, and ruby at the root chakra to stimulate feelings of ambition, will, and determination; to boost confidence; for leadership; and for grounding.

Anger: While this anger protocol won't magically dissolve your clients' anger, it will help them to connect with the feeling from a place of mindfulness so that they can learn from its message, and it can then be released. Once anger is heard, it tends to fade on its own. Place amethyst in the receptive hand or on the third eye chakra for mindfulness, honey calcite on the solar plexus to help balance the energy of that chakra and to diminish feelings of blockage or resistance, and chrysocolla on the throat chakra or in the dominant hand to help cool the emotional body and increase feelings of compassion.

Anxiety: Place blue lace agate in the receptive hand to calm, soothe, and center; smoky quartz in the dominant hand to relieve stress and pent-up energy; lithium quartz on the heart chakra to reduce feelings of anxiety; and angelite on the third eye chakra to help calm the mind.

Boundaries, affirming healthy:
Place amazonite on the throat
chakra, green aventurine on the
heart chakra, sunstone and tiger's
eye on the solar plexus, and ruby
at the root chakra.

Breaking bad habits: Place
amethyst on the third eye chakra,
unakite on the heart chakra,
hematite on the root chakra,
sodalite in the receptive hand,
smoky quartz in the dominant hand,
and apache tear at the root chakra.

Calm: In general, placing any light
blue, gray, lavender, or pink crystal
on the body or in the hands will help
to induce calm. For more specific
protocols, determine what is
causing your client not to feel calm,
and address that cause(s).

**Career changes, sudden or
scary:** Place rhodonite on the heart
chakra, honey calcite on the solar
plexus, and ruby on the root chakra.

**Childhood trauma, healing or
recovery from:** Place mangano
calcite, sugilite, malachite, and
pink kunzite on the heart chakra;
rhodochrosite on the solar plexus;

apache tear and snowflake
obsidian on the root chakra;
aragonite star cluster in the
receptive hand; and smoky elestial
quartz in the dominant hand.

Clarity: Most often, when a client is
saying she needs clarity, she usually
means something else. It could
be a better sense of herself, what
she's feeling or what she wants,
which direction to head in or what
choice she should make, whom to
trust, and so on. Inquire as to what
she truly means and is seeking,
and then address that issue with
the relevant protocols. If you feel
that your client may be resisting
or in denial, place sodalite on her
third eye chakra, rose quartz on her
heart, and apache tear at her root.

Communication: If your client is
feeling blocked in communicating
feelings, place blue calcite on his
throat chakra to help clear the
blockage. If he's feeling afraid to
speak up, place aquamarine on the
throat chakra or in the receptive
hand. If your client is struggling to
articulate or present concepts and
ideas, place blue kyanite on his
throat or third eye chakra.

Compassion: To help your client feel more compassion for herself and others, and to communicate more softly, place chrysocolla on the throat chakra for compassion and ease of expression; rose quartz, malachite, and mangano calcite at the heart chakra for self-love, healing of emotional wounds, and gentleness; and apache tear at the root to help heal any childhood wounding that may be related to fear, shame, or grief as a contributing factor.

Courage: Place amethyst on the third eye chakra to shift from negative thinking; aquamarine at the throat for courage and emotional cool; rhodonite at the heart chakra for courageous love; citrine at the solar plexus for confidence and energy; and hematite at the root chakra for grounding, fortitude, and resilience. You can also draw a clockwise cho ku rei into every chakra from the heart to the root for added strength.

Creativity: Place blue quartz at the throat to help energize the chakra and increase creative flow of expression; and carnelian, orange calcite, and fire agate on the sacral chakra to clear any blockage in creative energy, stimulate and sustain desire, and spark inspiration.

Depression: Place amethyst in the receptive hand to help shift and heal negative patterns of thought and expectation, citrine in the dominant hand to help lift the spirits, ametrine or sugilite on the third eye chakra for mental healing, and rose quartz or morganite and watermelon tourmaline at the heart chakra for emotional healing and recovery.

Determination: Place tiger iron at the solar plexus to stimulate will and increase feelings of determination and fortitude, and onyx and red jasper at the root chakra for added energy, steadfastness, and grounding.

Discipline, commitment: Many people associate punishment and restriction with the word *discipline*, so I prefer to use the word *commitment*, as it feels more empowering. Place rhodonite or eudialyte at the heart chakra to help your client make loving, heart-centered choices; and onyx or vanadinite at the root chakra for added feelings of commitment, determination, grounding, and focus.

Expression, emotional: If your client is struggling to connect with or express his emotions or emotional needs, place amazonite on the throat to increase the flow of emotional energy between the heart and throat chakras, facilitating connection to emotional truth. Place rubellite at the heart chakra for love and depth, and carnelian at the sacral chakra for empowerment and emotional fortitude. Place one hand on the heart chakra and the other over the throat simultaneously while channeling reiki.

Fear: Place apophyllite at the crown chakra to help unplug from the ego and the fear-based self, amethyst at the third eye to shift negative thinking and calm stress or anxiety, blue lace agate at the throat for cooling and centering of the emotional self, spirit quartz on the heart chakra for courage and to combat feelings of fear, and

aragonite star cluster on the solar plexus for increased confidence and feelings of leadership.

Focus: Place fluorite on the third eye chakra or in the receptive hand to help stimulate the mind and reason, and onyx on the root chakra or in the dominant hand for grounding and increased sense of focus.

Forgiveness: Place chrysocolla on the throat chakra for compassionate communication; mangano calcite, morganite, and pink kunzite on the heart chakra for acceptance, compassion, and empathy; chrysoprase for compassion and altruism; and rhodochrosite for the healing of any old wounds on the solar plexus chakra.

Grief: Place angelite and angel aura quartz at the crown chakra for serenity and peace; aquamarine at the throat for courage and soothing of the emotional body; mangano calcite, rhodochrosite, and morganite at the heart for deep emotional healing and release; and apache tear at the root or in the receptive hand for recovery from the sense of loss and grief.

Happiness: Place peridot and pink kunzite on the heart chakra for greater feelings of joy, optimism, and abundance; sunstone and ocean jasper on the solar plexus for confidence, optimism, and ease; and citrine on the sacral chakra for grounding in the emotional body and positivity.

Heartbreak: To help your client heal from loss or heartbreak, place malachite, rhodochrosite, rose quartz, and rhodonite on the heart chakra to help him emotionally release, and engage in the process of healing emotional wounding, feeling self-love, and having courage to love again. You can place mangano calcite in his receptive hand for acceptance or letting go, and watermelon tourmaline in his dominant hand for a greater sense of emotional well-being overall.

Memory: To help your client improve her memory, or to help her retrieve memories, first hold a piece of clear quartz in your dominant hand while focusing on that intention, and then place it in your client's receptive hand or on her third eye chakra to help send that energy into her mental field. As an alternative, you can place sodalite, blue kyanite, and fluorite on the third eye to help empower that chakra and stimulate memory, and onyx on the root to help ground and focus the intention. You can also draw a clockwise cho ku rei into the third eye for empowerment and healing.

Mood swings: Place bloodstone and orange calcite at the sacral chakra to help balance the chakra, clear any blockage, and stabilize the emotional field.

Negative thought patterns: Place amethyst and sodalite at the third eye chakra to help your client shift from negative patterns of thought, and to help him come to a greater level of inner awareness; rubellite at the heart chakra for empowered self-love; and hematite and black obsidian at the root to help ground your client in his intention and bring any relevant shadow beliefs to the surface so they can be addressed.

Nightmares: To help bring your client relief from nightmares, first clear her aura (see "Aura Clearing and Healing Protocols"), and then, to help her understand the meaning of her nightmares, place elestial quartz in her receptive hand for high-frequency light and healing; azurite and optical calcite on the third eye chakra for insight and to divine meaning; and watermelon tourmaline on the heart chakra to help settle the emotional field. You may also suggest that your client clear the energy in her home or bedroom.

Optimism: Place citrine and ocean jasper on the solar plexus for brightness, ease, and a more positive perspective; green aventurine on the heart chakra for vitality and receptivity; optical calcite on the third eye if he needs to adopt a new perspective; or amethyst to help him make a shift in thought patterns if he's mired in negative thinking.

Overwhelm, emotional: Place selenite, lithium quartz, and mangano calcite over the heart chakra to help lift and dissolve dense energy or emotional feelings of heaviness, to soothe anxiety, and create more feelings of serenity. Put blue lace agate and aquamarine at the throat to help calm and center the emotional body; and smoky quartz at the root chakra and in both hands to help ground, stabilize, and clear stress from the system. You can draw a raku along the body from the crown to the feet to help clear excess emotional energy from the system and ground it in the Earth.

Overwhelm, mental: Place smoky elestial quartz at the crown to help draw more wisdom and perspective from the higher self into the body; fluorite and blue sapphire at the third eye for mental order, reason, and balance; blue lace agate at the throat to calm, center, and collect mental energy; and onyx and tiger iron at the root to help your client feel more grounded, present, and empowered.

Pleasure, passion, or desire:
If your client is having difficulty experiencing physical or emotional pleasure, or if she feels blocked from her sense of passion or desire on any level, first be sure to ascertain the underlying causes and address them accordingly. I've often found that the problem wasn't that a client was blocked in experiencing pleasure, or lacking in passion or desire, but that deep down she was trying to feel something that she didn't authentically feel. For example, it could be that she's no longer in love with her partner, she's on the wrong career path, a project's no longer resonating for her, or that something simply isn't turning her on. In cases like these, people have a tendency to blame themselves for what's not working instead of facing the possibility that they need to make changes or new choices. That being said, to help stimulate the sacral chakra and increase feelings of pleasure, passion, or desire, place ruby, garnet, and carnelian on the sacral chakra, and rhodochrosite on the heart chakra.

Relaxation: In general, any pale blue, pink, lavender, white, gray, or pale-green crystals placed in the hands or on the heart chakra will help a person relax.

Self-love, self-worth: If I had to pinpoint two of the most common underlying causes of people's negative self-image, limiting fears or beliefs, or inability to succeed or prosper, heal emotionally, or find love, it would be a lack of self-love and self-worth. Ultimately, the motivation for every choice we make can be whittled down to either fear or love. The more we love ourselves, the more worthy we feel, the more we are able to make loving, empowered, honest, and productive choices. To help your client heal and reclaim deeper, authentic feelings of self-love and self-worth, place rhodochrosite, rose quartz, and rhodonite at the heart chakra for heart healing, compassion, forgiveness, acceptance, courage, and pure love energy; and ruby at the root chakra for empowered self-leadership, grounding, passion, strength, and confidence. You can also place rose quartz in both hands.

Shadow self, healing: To help your client uncover aspects of her shadow self, including resistance, denial, fear-based commitments, and limiting or negative beliefs, so that they can be acknowledged, resolved, and healed, place covelite, black obsidian, or apache tear at the root chakra to help bring shadow aspects to the surface of your client's consciousness; sodalite on the third eye for insight, inner truth, and self-awareness; and rose quartz on the heart chakra for self-love.

Wisdom: To help your client access higher levels of wisdom from his own consciousness or higher self, place scolecite and apophyllite at the crown chakra for tranquility, access to higher consciousness, and greater receptivity; blue kyanite and optical calcite at the third eye chakra for increased insight, memory, and reason; and aragonite star cluster in the receptive hand to help establish a stronger connection to the soul's love and wisdom.

> **IMPORTANT NOTE:**
> Never engage your client in shadow healing or use shadow healing protocols without her knowledge and consent. If shadow aspects are brought to the surface that your client is not willingly prepared to deal with, it can have damaging consquences on her psyche and emotional well-being.

SPIRITUAL GROWTH AND HEALING

What compels many people to first work with crystals is that they can activate psychic and spiritual abilities. I tell my students and clients that stronger intuition, more active dream states, a greater sense of faith, and strengthened psychic abilities are all a natural by-product of working with crystal energy. It just happens. Perhaps it's the exposure to higher, natural frequencies and vibrations that activate something in our own energy matrix, or maybe it's that they're gifts sent to us from the Divine to help us evolve. No matter the reason, it's something I've observed time and time again and it always seems to hold true.

Psychic Abilities

Even though I grew up with psychic abilities, I never really understood them or knew what they meant. I honestly thought that my eyes just went funny in the woods or at night, and that when I'd see or feel strange things and the hairs on the back of my neck would go up, I was just a victim of my own overactive imagination. I remember a friend of mine, a psychic medium, sharing with me at dinner one night that she had begun to see energy. She described seeing bubbles and lines and dots, rainbow swirls, orbs, colored mists, and sparkles of light, and I said to her: "*That's* what that is?! Energy? Then I've been seeing energy my whole life!" Early on in my healing career, I was obsessed with activating and strengthening my psychic abilities, so I was shocked to realize that I'd had them all along and just hadn't paid any attention to them. That happens with a lot of people, and I think it's because of our expectations: Sometimes we expect our psychic abilities to be the way they're portrayed in the movies—seeing things with technicolor clarity and knowing things in minute detail before they happen. For most of us, our abilities are more subtle, but they become stronger when we pay attention to them without expectation.

I'd been working with crystals regularly to help open my third eye chakra, a common expression used in spiritual circles that means awakening your psychic abilities. There are many forms of psychic ability, but I was focused on the four main categories: (1) clairvoyance, the ability to see beyond the physical reality of our world, including future or distant events; (2) clairsentience, the ability to sense or feel subtle energy; (3) clairaudience, being able to hear beyond the normal human range of hearing, including sounds or messages from spirits or other realms; and (4) claircognizance, the ability to innately know, understand, or spontaneously receive psychic information in your mind. I wanted them all and, through experimentation, I was figuring out which crystals worked best for developing each ability.

I'm a great believer that every living soul has intuition. Every person has psychic abilities; it's just a matter of developing them and understanding that some may be stronger than others. In time, I've developed all of mine into strengths with one exception: clairaudience. It startles me to hear things that are out of the norm, especially at night. So I tend to block that ability. Which brings me to a point: I've found that the three main things that block the opening and development of our psychic abilities are fear, doubt, and pressure. If you're afraid of what you might experience, you'll subconsciously block it from happening. If you doubt what you're seeing or sensing, your conscious mind will begin to filter it out. And if you're putting yourself under too much pressure to have a psychic experience, there's likely a subconscious fear or doubt at play that can then block your ability in a particular area. Approaching your ability with curiosity, allowing it to blossom, and then paying attention to it are your three main allies in psychic development.

CASE STUDY: Annie

Annie was living in a shelter. She'd moved to New York to be closer to her daughter, but then had lost her job, her apartment, and had only succeeded in finding a part-time job when she booked a session to see me. She shared that she'd had a spiritual epiphany, that the losses she had experienced were meant to clear the decks, and that it was time for her to pursue her path as a spiritual healer. In a dream, she had been guided to find a reiki master who could open her third eye chakra, and when she happened upon my website in an online search, she knew I was the one. She believed that with enhanced psychic ability, and a clear connection to the Divine, she would be guided on her new path and her life would begin to turn around. Having been through a similar experience myself, and having worked with crystals to help me through my own transition, I could see why she'd turned up on my doorstep!

Here's an example of a Crystal Reiki layout I would use for Annie, incorporating the life-purpose, crown chakra–expanding, and third eye–activating protocols:

Root Chakra: Ruby and Smoky Quartz

Sacral Chakra: Fire Opal

Solar Plexus: Citrine

Heart: Eudialyte

Throat: Aquamarine

Third Eye: Moldavite

Crown: Selenite, Apophyllite, Scolecite, and a Single-Terminated Quartz Point

Hands: Selenite

At the end of the session, Annie sat up from my reiki table with such a look of serenity and softness, as if she were glowing peacefully from within. I said to her, "I think things are going to get better for you now." She smiled, nodded her head, and said, "I know they are." I offered to waive her fee, given her circumstances, but again she smiled and thrust the payment in my hand. I had to admire the way she walked out of my healing space: self-assured, strong, and fearless. I lost touch with Annie, but I don't doubt for a second that she's out there doing great work somewhere, and that the world's a better place for it. And I'm grateful.

CRYSTAL KEY

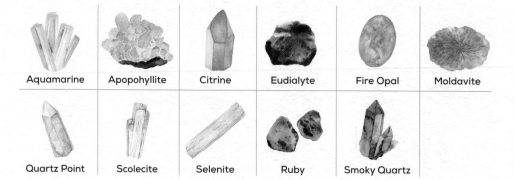

Aquamarine	Apopohyllite	Citrine	Eudialyte	Fire Opal	Moldavite
Quartz Point	Scolecite	Selenite	Ruby	Smoky Quartz	

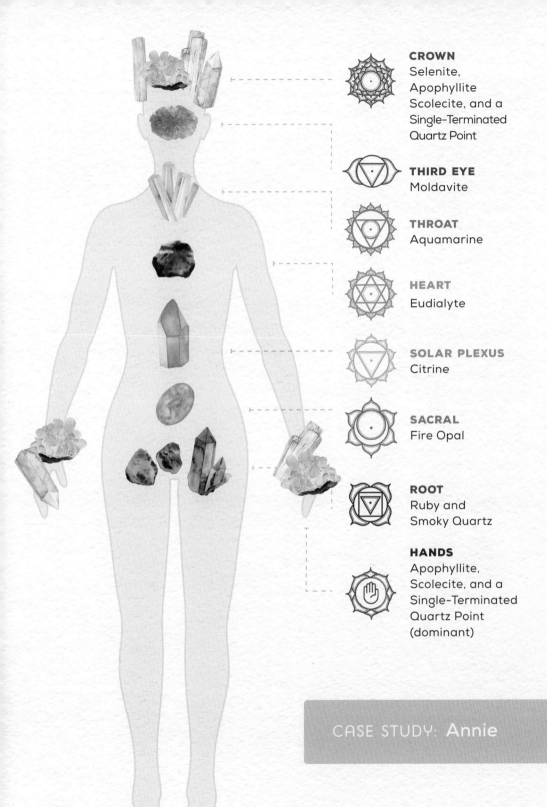

CROWN
Selenite,
Apophyllite
Scolecite, and a
Single-Terminated
Quartz Point

THIRD EYE
Moldavite

THROAT
Aquamarine

HEART
Eudialyte

SOLAR PLEXUS
Citrine

SACRAL
Fire Opal

ROOT
Ruby and
Smoky Quartz

HANDS
Apophyllite,
Scolecite, and a
Single-Terminated
Quartz Point
(dominant)

CASE STUDY: Annie

Karmic, Life-Purpose, and Past-Life Healing

Of course, spiritual healing doesn't only refer to the opening of psychic abilities; it encompasses a wide range and variety of areas and issues. Common topics that would show up on my healing table include karmic healing (the balancing and resolving of unfortunate karma), past-life healing, and seeking out meaning or purpose in life. Spiritual healing at this level can go deep and may be complicated, and, in some cases, can even be a lifelong process. Once again you need to tread carefully so you're not putting yourself in a position where you're being expected to provide answers or solutions. As a Crystal Reiki healer, your job is to help provide the energy your clients need to help them discover their own answers, and work toward their own solutions.

CASE STUDY:
Cynthia

Cynthia wanted karmic healing. She'd had a very difficult life, and no matter how much she tried, she could never seem to keep a friend or a job for long. Every time she felt as if things were starting to turn around for her and get better, she said she'd be hit by the Universe and end up back in the dumps again. She craved simple things: love, a family, community, rewarding work that provided a decent living, and faith. She shared that she'd felt angry toward God for a long time, believing that the Divine was unjust and to blame for her misfortune and pain. She had worked with therapists, career coaches, and life coaches, to no real avail, and felt that there must be past-life karma that she was atoning for in this lifetime.

Cases like Cynthia's are challenging, because it's a matter of supporting your client in figuring out what is being manifested by the shadow self in this lifetime, and what is surfacing from the wounds of previous lifetimes. We had to work with a lot of mental and emotional healing protocols, including the shadow self, childhood trauma, and self-worth protocols. We also worked on raising Cynthia's energy frequency by expanding her crown chakra, so that she could start accessing higher, divine guidance, and to help enhance the past-life regression work she was doing with another practitioner. We also incorporated some transformational work at the root chakra to help her balance or shift related issues to family, stability, and abundance. And, finally, we put in place the karmic-healing protocol to support her in making more soul-aligned choices in her daily life.

Here's an example of the Crystal Reiki layout I would use for Cynthia, incorporating the shadow-self, self-worth, transformation, and karmic-healing protocols:

Root: Moldavite, Black Obsidian, and Apache Tear

Sacral: Bloodstone

Solar Plexus: Rhodochrosite and Honey Calcite

Heart: Rose Quartz, Rhodochrosite, and Rhodonite

Throat: Aquamarine

Third Eye: Sodalite and Astrophyllite

Crown: Apophyllite

Hands: Scolecite (receptive), Smoky Elestial Quartz (dominant)

It took a village to help Cynthia heal, including working with the aforementioned past-life regressionist, a psychic healer, and a new therapist, along with her own will and faith. Working with the crystals helped to expand her own psychic and spiritual abilities, and, along with the healing love energy of her heart chakra and the transformative vibes of the moldavite, she finally was making strides forward. She had begun to despair that her life would never turn around, but it just needed a lot of work and the help of a few good people (and many great crystals!). She scored a job she could manage, found a meditation group that provided some of the support and community she needed, and was back out on the dating scene feeling more empowered in who she was and what she was worth. When the decision is made to heal, healing is inevitable.

CRYSTAL KEY

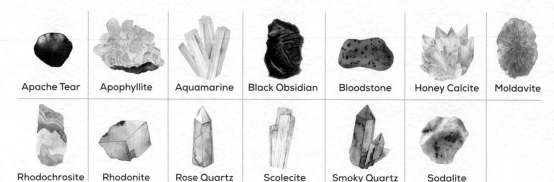

| Apache Tear | Apophyllite | Aquamarine | Black Obsidian | Bloodstone | Honey Calcite | Moldavite |

| Rhodochrosite | Rhodonite | Rose Quartz | Scolecite | Smoky Quartz | Sodalite |

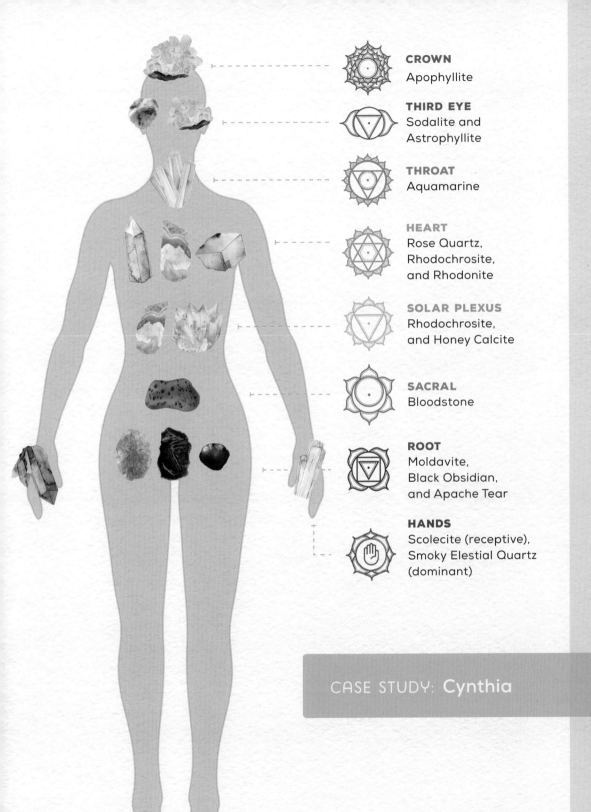

CROWN
Apophyllite

THIRD EYE
Sodalite and
Astrophyllite

THROAT
Aquamarine

HEART
Rose Quartz,
Rhodochrosite,
and Rhodonite

SOLAR PLEXUS
Rhodochrosite,
and Honey Calcite

SACRAL
Bloodstone

ROOT
Moldavite,
Black Obsidian,
and Apache Tear

HANDS
Scolecite (receptive),
Smoky Elestial Quartz
(dominant)

CASE STUDY: Cynthia

SPIRITUAL HEALING PROTOCOLS

Place the following crystals as described. Use reiki hand placements and protocols as you feel guided, or as indicated.

Abundance: Place green garnet, moss agate, or green aventurine on the heart chakra for feelings of expansiveness, receptivity, and abundance. Place citrine on the solar plexus for increased confidence, attraction of prosperity, and optimism; and place chrysanthemum stone in the receptive hand to strengthen the attraction of good fortune and to help instill a positive mind-set.

Amplifying flow of reiki healing energy: Place mangano calcite, danburite, healer's gold, apophylite, or infinite under your reiki table to amplify and strengthen the healing flow of energy in your healing space. You can also wear any one of these crystals to help amplify and strengthen your own reiki during a session.

Angelic communication: Place angel aura quartz for hope and faith, angelite for angelic connection, and danburite for increased frequency at the crown chakra. You can add seraphinite at the heart for loving communion with the angels and to welcome pure angelic guidance.

Ascended master, communication with: To help your client connect with an ascended master's presence, wisdom, or guidance, place healer's gold in her receptive hand, selenite in her dominant hand, and gold rutilated quartz and apophylite at the crown to help raise her frequencies and facilitate her connection to the ascended master realm. This protocol will also help to enhance your client's ability to receive telepathic communication.

Chakras, clearing blockages in: In general, calcites help to clear and dissolve energy blockages. They are slower in vibration so they run a low risk of throwing a chakra out of balance; they steadily yet gently emit healing energy. You can match the color of the calcite to the relevant chakra so that the crystals resonate on similar frequencies: red calcite for the root, orange calcite for the sacral, honey calcite for the solar plexus, green calcite for the heart, blue calcite for the throat, and clear calcite for the third eye and crown chakras. Clear calcite can be safely placed on all chakras.

Chakras, energizing: Quartz and quartz-based crystals help to energize the chakras by channeling more healing chi and increasing the flow of healing chi through a chakra. You can match the color of the quartz to the relevant chakra so that the crystals resonate on similar frequencies: smoky quartz at the root, carnelian at the sacral, citrine at the solar plexus, rose quartz at the heart, blue quartz at the throat, amethyst on the third eye, clear quartz at the crown. You can also place a double-terminated quartz point on any chakra to help energize and increase the healing flow of chi in both directions through the chakra.

Channeling messages from spirits: Place selenite or danburite at the crown to raise your client's frequency, which helps him to access higher realms, spirits, and guidance. Angelite on the throat helps enhance spirit communication, seraphinite at the heart helps to maintain only loving connections, and clear quartz points (pointing up) in both hands helps to amplify and magnify the energy of the intention, while also increasing psychic ability and clarifying communication.

Connection to Earth spirits and elementals: If your client wants to be able to see or interact with fairies and other nature spirits (including the spirits of medicinal plants and herbs), place green apophyllite and spirit quartz on her heart chakra, infinite at her root, staurolyte in her receptive hand, and chiastolite in her dominant hand. All these crystals help to strengthen our connection to the nature spirit realm, provide protection from harm and mischief, and enhance our ability to see, hear, and sense those spirits.

Crown chakra, expanding: Expanding your client's crown chakra can activate spiritual awakening and growth, enhance his connection to higher realms, spirits, and his higher self, as well as support past-life memory work and karmic awareness. Place selenite in both hands and at the crown chakra to help dissolve any energy blockage and increase the level of your client's frequency. Add scolecite for harmony and wisdom; apophyllite to help him detach from his fear-based ego; a single-terminated quartz crystal pointing up from the crown chakra to help send his spiritual awareness toward his higher self, other realms, or other dimensions; and smoky quartz at the root to help him maintain his connection to his body, and to help ground and stabilize all of the crystal energy.

Distance reiki: Channel reiki through a quartz point, or a selenite tower with the point facing away from you, into an apophyllite point directed upward, or while holding danburite in your dominant hand to help amplify, magnify, and direct reiki to your recipient(s).

Divine feminine: If your client is seeking to be more in tune with the divine feminine consciousness, or if she wishes to cultivate more of her own feminine energy, place larimar at the throat chakra, moonstone at the crown, silver rutilated quartz in the receptive hand, and thulite or rose quartz at the heart chakra. All these crystals resonate with the divine feminine frequencies, and the thulite or rose quartz helps to create a more loving, receptive space for those frequencies to enter.

Divine masculine: If your client is seeking to be more in tune with the divine masculine consciousness, or if he wishes to cultivate more of his own masculine energy, place healer's gold at the crown chakra, chalcopyrite or pyrite at the heart chakra, and citrine at the solar plexus. All these crystals vibrate on similar frequencies to that of the divine masculine, and the citrine helps to create a more active and vital space for those frequencies to be embodied.

Dreaming, enhanced: If your client is feeling blocked in her dreaming, having difficulty remembering her dreams, or if she's seeking to develop a stronger practice of dream work, place labradorite, fluorite, and Herkimer diamond on the third eye chakra to help stimulate dreaming capability and enhance visual memory, and moonstone and elestial quartz at the crown to help increase safe access to the dream state and dream planes of consciousness.

Faith: To help boost your client's sense of faith, place selenite and angel aura quartz at the crown chakra or in the hands, and mangano calcite on the heart chakra for gentle acceptance, love, and compassion.

Higher heart activation: An integral part of growing and evolving as a spiritual being is the willingness to experience deeper, more authentic levels of unconditional love, gratitude, and oneness. Place on the heart chakra pink kunzite for divine love and joy, seraphinite for greater feelings of wholeness, and emerald for unconditional love and expansion.

Higher self, connection to: Place pink kunzite and rubellite at the heart chakra for divine love and loving energy, chrysocolla at the throat to form a sacred connection, Herkimer diamond on the third eye for enhanced psychic ability and communication, and apophyllite and scolecite at the crown chakra to strengthen the bond of light between your client and his higher self.

Karma, healing: Misunderstanding and misinformation abound when it comes to karma. I personally do not subscribe to the belief that karma is the Universe's axe-wielding way of delivering punishment and exacting vengeance. Rather, it's providing opportunities in our lives to make different choices that are more in alignment with our souls, as opposed to past situations where we made choices out of fear. As we make that soul-aligned choice, the karma has served its purpose and dissolves. It sounds simple enough, but it can take lifetimes of healing and experience to finally be able to make that soul-aligned choice. If your client feels she is in need of karmic healing, place astrophyllite on her third eye for inner wisdom and to tap into soul-based information; apophyllite at her crown to help her detach from fear-based thinking and connect with her higher self; scolecite in her receptive hand for higher wisdom, and elestial quartz in her dominant hand to help clear lower energy and support her in karmic healing.

Life purpose, discovering: The hard part about discovering our life purpose is what people expect. From my own experience and my work in the Akashic records, a soul's purpose in a given lifetime often centers on what needs to be learned or healed, more so than the job that's worked or the legacy that's left behind. Viewing a vocation or a great achievement as someone's life purpose strikes me as more of a modern idea, yet that doesn't negate those possibilities. I do believe that we are all here for a purpose, and having a sense of that purpose can help provide comfort and help us to navigate through some of life's more challenging moments. To help your client access the soul-based and divine wisdom he needs to discover his life purpose, place celestite at the crown chakra for spiritual awakening and activation, unakite at the heart to help bridge the gap between his spiritual and physical selves, elestial quartz in his receptive hand for access to higher divine and karmic knowledge, and ajoite in his dominant hand for evolution or moldavite for transformation.

Life purpose, following: Once your client has an awareness or understanding of her life purpose, she may feel unclear as to how or where to begin, and daunted by shadow-based doubts and limiting beliefs. Place eudialyte or rhodonite over the heart chakra to help ground her desire to pursue her purpose in the physical realm, and ruby and rhodonite at the root chakra to help empower and anchor her in her sense of purpose. For shadow issues, use the *Shadow self, healing* protocol on page 138.

Intuition boosters: You can place shiva lingam, amethyst, ajoite, citrine, tiger's eye, holly blue agate, merlinite, sugilite, azurite, quartz, blue kyanite, fluorite (purple), moldavite, or Herkimer diamond either in your client's receptive hand, or on his third eye chakra to help boost, clarify, or enhance his intuition.

Manifestation: If you're going to help attune your client's energy to more potent frequencies of manifestation, be sure she understands that she'll need to be mindful of how she thinks, what she feels, and what she wishes for! I used this protocol repeatedly for clients and it always works, but if your client is perpetually in a negative mind-set or operating from a fear-based place, she should work on shifting that first; otherwise, she'll end of manifesting more misery. Place epidote in her receptive hand and clear topaz in her dominant hand, which helps to accelerate the manifestation process; pyrite on the solar plexus to help manifest on the physical plane; blue apatite on the throat to increase vocal manifestation (speaking something out loud so it happens); and optical calcite on the third eye chakra to help shift perspective to possibility and accelerate the manifestation of the visualization process.

Prosperity, attraction: To help your client attract greater levels of prosperity, place lemurian jade in his receptive hand; golden topaz, pyrite, and citrine on the solar plexus; and chrysanthemum stone in his dominant hand.

Psychic abilities, clairaudience: Place cavansite, blue tourmaline, azurite, or chrysocolla on the throat chakra.

Psychic abilities, claircognizance: Place apophyllite, moldavite, labradorite, scolecite, selenite, ajoite, or elestial quartz at the crown chakra.

Psychic abilities, clairsentience: Place tiger's eye, citrine, honey calcite, or clear quartz on the solar plexus chakra.

Psychic abilities, clairvoyance: Place holly blue agate, lapis lazuli, sugilite, Herkimer diamond, moldavite, or azurite on the third eye chakra.

Relationship to God, healing: I tread lightly in including this because, while I felt guided to share this protocol, I do it knowing that readers of this book walk all paths of faith, religion, belief, and all are welcome! I consider myself to be pagan, but I do believe in a higher consciousness that I refer to as God, and a higher consciousness of the life principle that I refer to as Goddess. Due to experiences of pain and suffering I've experienced both in this life and in past lifetimes, I've had my own fair share of healing to do with my relationships to

God and Goddess, and I've had clients seeking to engage in a similar process. Place celestite, danburite, and apophyllite at the crown chakra to help increase your client's healing connection to the Divine; sugilite on the third eye to help heal past-life wounding; chrysocolla on the throat for sacred connection, communication, and compassion; and rubellite and emerald on the heart chakra for deep emotional healing and a greater sense of unconditional love and wholeness.

Spiritual awakening or growth: See *Crown chakra, expanding.*

Third eye chakra, activation: Place moldavite on the third eye chakra.

Transformation: Place moldavite on the chakra that most relates to the area in which your client is seeking transformation. For example, place it on the heart chakra to transform a loving relationship, on the root to transform a health-related issue, or on the solar plexus to transform a relationship to money or prosperity.

Aura Clearing, Shielding, and Healing

Last, but not least, we come to clearing, shielding, and healing the aura. I did so much energy-clearing work in New York City that it quickly became a known specialty of mine. Clients would come in saying that they felt "toxic," they had taken on so much negative energy from their friends, workplaces, the subway, their families, or horrible bosses that they could no longer function like themselves. I also worked with clients who had picked up spirit attachments from places like hospitals, cemeteries, old or institutional buildings, or who felt they had fallen victim to curses and hexes. At times I have had to undo the damage wrought by other people's botched shamanic rituals and Ayahuasca ceremonies gone wrong.

Much of what I learned about energy clearing and shielding came from the experience of having to do my own. The truth is, as an empathic and telepathic spiritual healer working and living in New York City,

I suffered greatly. In the early days, I took on a lot of my clients' energy, and I was constantly feeling bombarded, assaulted, and overwhelmed by the energy of the city. One of my reiki teachers once told me that the more your inner light grows and expands, the more you attract the dark. She wasn't kidding: Seeing dark things out of the corner of my eyes, tussling with malevolent spirits in my dreams at night, and getting hit with parasitic cords, psychic attachments, and energy vampires became too regular an experience for me.

I knew about energy clearing, using sage or a selenite stick to clear the energy of my aura, but I hadn't learned much about how to shield my energy effectively, or how to heal damage done to my aura from cords and spirit attachments. I remember one time where I'd been feeling off for a couple of weeks. I was tired and grumpy all the time, my intuition felt foggy, it was challenging to channel healing energy, and I was feeling less and less like myself. I finally had a breakdown: I couldn't get out of bed, I had no motivation to take care of myself, and I couldn't stop crying. At that point my inner voice, what I refer to as my "guidance," shot through me like a bolt: "You need help. Something's not right. You've taken on dark energy." Desperate, I called a shaman friend of mine, knowing that she usually booked up days in advance, and found that she'd just had a last-minute cancellation, and could see me for an energy-clearing session that afternoon. Coincidence? I think not!

By the time I reached her office a part of me had gone into denial and was thinking, "I'm OK. I don't really need this healing. I shouldn't have bothered." I've learned to never trust that voice of denial, because I've learned it's a ploy dark energy or spirits will use to try to keep you from seeking out help. They feed off your light, and they don't want to lose you as a source of energy. My friend spent three hours working on me that afternoon, clearing all kinds of parasitic cords and spirit attachments that were stuck to me. I walked out of there feeling better than I had in weeks, and determined to learn how to take proper energy care of myself.

As these things go, the more I focused on my own aura clearing, shielding, and healing, the more I attracted clients who needed the same help. I became what one friend of mine referred to as a "hound," being able to sniff out and detect psychic cords, harmful spirit attachments, or dark, heavy energy on people the second they walked through the door. Let me be clear: This is not glamorous work; in fact, it can be risky if you don't know what you're doing.

The great thing about working with crystals is that you don't have to do a whole lot; they'll do the bulk of the work for you if you work with the right ones in the right places. You can step out of the way and let the crystal frequencies do the repelling, clearing, healing, and shielding work for you. If you've done your prep work properly, any risk to your own energy should be minimal.

Reminder: It's all just energy. Psychic cords are fairly benign; they're just draining because they're unhealthy energy attachments between people and things. Clients most often create their own thought-forms (imagine a bubble filled with negative energy that's corded or tethered to your client's aura) by fixating too much—often on their fears, worries, anger, etc. —and those thought-forms follow them around like dark, little clouds. Anything more intense than that falls out of the scope of this book. Anything super-intense falls out of *my* scope altogether!

Keep in mind that if any of this is making you feel uncomfortable, you don't have to do it. If a client comes to see you and you suspect she's got dark energy on her, and that pushes you too far out of your comfort zone, it is 100 percent OK to honor your boundaries and refer her to another practitioner. Even in trainings, I've had students who have refused to learn about some of this because they're afraid of attracting it into their experience, and I've never forced it on them. If you feel that way, you can skip this next part and jump to either the aura-clearing protocols at the end of this chapter or to Part 4.

CASE STUDY:
Maria

I remember the very first time I encountered a thought-form attachment on a client. Maria had been in South America visiting a world-famous shaman and healer, only to come back with something dark attached to her aura. She came to see me for a Crystal Reiki session, and I knew something felt off right from the start. It literally felt like the reiki energy was being blocked from flowing into Maria's system. My intuition was also feeling really fuzzy and unclear, and when I scanned her aura, I noticed this huge mass of what felt like static energy floating just over her body. I asked her how she was feeling, and Maria broke down into tears and said, "I don't feel like myself."

I immediately lit up my smudge stick and started sage-ing Maria's aura, and then feeling along her aura and chakras for signs of a psychic cord. Typically, entities or thought-forms will parasitically attach themselves to a person's aura so that they can siphon off the person's energy. I had been taught how to sever psychic cords using my hands in my reiki master training, but that didn't feel safe to me, so I picked up my selenite stick and intuitively swung it through the cord, severing the connection. I felt for it again, and it had been broken. I then channeled reiki through the selenite stick to help dissolve any remaining energy from the cord in Maria's aura.

I was concerned that the thought-form would still be floating around in the room, so I scanned with my intuitive senses until I found a spot that felt very dense and heavy with dark energy. Then I drew a big Tibetan dai ko myo in the air and pushed it with reiki toward the spot. I have no idea where the thought-form went—I'm assuming up into the light—but, thankfully, after that it was cleared and it never bothered Maria again. Amazingly, even though her eyes were covered with an eye pillow and she had no idea what I was doing, Maria gave a deep sigh of relief right after the spot had been cleared and said to me, "It's gone, isn't it?" She could automatically sense the difference.

I added one of the aura-healing crystal protocols listed below to Maria's crystal layout, channeled some reiki into the areas of her aura that felt as if they had holes or were weak, and then continued with the healing session as usual.

Here's a sample layout for Maria using the aura-clearing and -shielding protocols:

Root: Bloodstone and Smoky Quartz

Sacral: Black Obsidian and Aragonite Star Cluster

Solar Plexus: Healer's Gold and Infinite

Heart: Spirit Quartz And Labradorite

Throat: Blue Kyanite

Third Eye: Fluorite And Amethyst

Crown: Tourmaline Quartz and Selenite

Hands: Selenite (receptive), Black Tourmaline (dominant)

CRYSTAL KEY

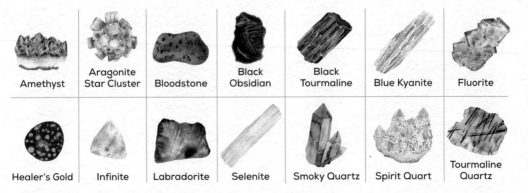

Amethyst	Aragonite Star Cluster	Bloodstone	Black Obsidian	Black Tourmaline	Blue Kyanite	Fluorite
Healer's Gold	Infinite	Labradorite	Selenite	Smoky Quartz	Spirit Quart	Tourmaline Quartz

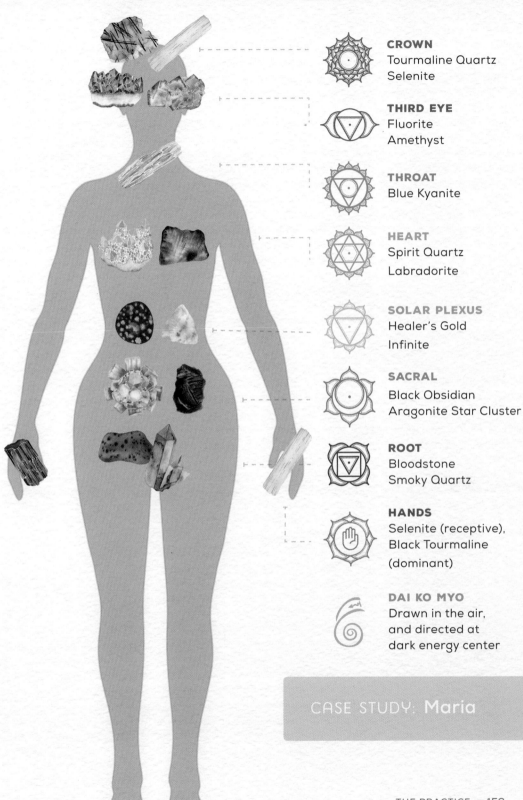

CROWN
Tourmaline Quartz
Selenite

THIRD EYE
Fluorite
Amethyst

THROAT
Blue Kyanite

HEART
Spirit Quartz
Labradorite

SOLAR PLEXUS
Healer's Gold
Infinite

SACRAL
Black Obsidian
Aragonite Star Cluster

ROOT
Bloodstone
Smoky Quartz

HANDS
Selenite (receptive),
Black Tourmaline
(dominant)

DAI KO MYO
Drawn in the air,
and directed at
dark energy center

CASE STUDY: Maria

From then on, I had more and more energy-clearing and -shielding work show up on my doorstep, particularly from other healers, psychics, intuitive readers and counselors, as well as massage therapists, yoga instructors, and other alternative healing practitioners. This is why I maintain that, even if you're not a spiritual healer, per se, but you work on a person's body or are exposed to his or her energy in a yoga class, it's still important to learn about aura clearing, healing, and shielding. Not only will it help you stay healthier longer, but it will keep you from having to spend money on seeing people like me!

Aura Clearing and Healing Protocols

Aura clearing: To clear the aura of psychic debris and lower frequencies, place tourmaline quartz at the crown for neutralizing and purification; spirit quartz at the heart chakra, which will repel psychic debris; selenite in the receptive hand to dissolve and purify dense or negative energy; black tourmaline in the dominant hand to repel and neutralize psychic debris; and smoky quartz or elestial quartz at the root chakra to clear it all from the system.

Aura clearing with a selenite stick: Pass a selenite stick through your client's aura, starting at the crown chakra, and slowly working down to her feet. Selenite will dissolve any blocked energy it encounters. If you feel a bump or a blockage as you go, pass the selenite back and forth through the blockage until it dissipates. Repeat on one side of the body, then the other, along her back, and then under her feet. You can do this with your client standing, or while lying on the table and either passing the stick under the table for her back, or leaving it under the table during the session.

Aura healing and strengthening: If you sense that your client's aura has been damaged by psychic cords, psychic attack, or unhealthy lifestyle choices, place spirit quartz on his heart chakra, infinite on his solar plexus, and aragonite star cluster on his sacral chakra, which will all help to heal and repair the aura while strengthening the body's electromagnetic field. Add bloodstone to the root chakra to help ground and revitalize your client's energy.

Aura shielding and protection: To increase your client's natural energy defenses, or to help create an energy shield around his aura, place selenite at his crown chakra for purification and to raise his frequency; fluorite at his third eye for cloaking; aqua aura quartz anywhere on his body to create a protective barrier; blue kyanite to repel dark spirits on his throat chakra; labradorite to create a shield at his heart; healer's gold to help protect his solar plexus; black obsidian at his sacral chakra to repel lower energies that could be attracted to the shadow self; and smoky quartz at his root to help clear psychic debris and lower, harmful energy from the body. You can also place amethyst in both his hands to help ward off dark energy, and to reduce fear or anxiety that might attract it.

Severing psychic cords: While the idea of severing psychic cords may sound like spiritual ninja work, it's actually a pretty straightforward process. Be sure that you've done your prep work properly so that you are adequately shielded and in your power; if not, you run the risk of a cord mistakenly attaching to you once you've cut it. If you're not sure or if this work makes you feel nervous, you can opt out of it and use the aura-clearing protocols above.

1. Scan your client's aura either clairvoyantly or with your hands to find where the cord is attached.

2. Cut through the cord three times with your selenite stick (three times just to be thorough).

3. Draw a counterclockwise cho ku rei into the area where the cord was attached to help remove any remaining part of the cord.

4. Draw a clockwise cho ku rei into the area where the cord was attached to help it heal and to seal in any holes in the aura.

Now that you have all this crystal information, you're most likely wondering how you incorporate it all into a session, or what you start with first. This next section will walk you through how to give a Crystal Reiki session from start to finish.

HOW TO GIVE A CRYSTAL REIKI SESSION

As far as modern crystal healing goes, we're still very much pioneers in this work. While we want to be of service as much as we can, we also need to proceed with safety and accountability in mind. People can have all kinds of reactions to crystal energy: Some may find it overwhelming; some may feel nothing at all. Some may experience a torrent of emotional release, while others may feel overly anxious during a session or despondent for a couple of days afterwards. When you allow your knowledge to work hand in hand with your intuition, and you've done your prep work, as outlined in Part 2, you can approach each session with a certain measure of confidence and humility, ready to be of service and to do your work.

When it comes to how many crystals you use in a session, I find it's always best to err on the side of caution and to stick to the "less is more" rule. It's never been my experience that you need to pile a ton of crystals on a person's body to help effect change or healing. If anything, that may overwhelm your client and counteract the good you're trying to do! I've often found that the right crystal, placed on the right chakra at just the right time, can be all the energy a person needs.

Depending on your client's needs, start with the basic chakra layout as instructed below, and then stick to a maximum of using two to three crystal protocols per session. If that feels like too much, use less. If your client has a ton of issues to address, ask her what her top two or three priorities are, and work on those first. She can always book additional sessions.

Session Structure from Beginning to End

1. Choose your crystals. Begin by placing your basic chakra layout, first by referring to the chart on page 167, and then by placing your specific crystal protocols. Always place crystals on the body starting at the root and building up so that you keep your client grounded, and begin by placing physical healing protocols first as they're working at an energy level of greater density.

2. Call in your reiki.

3. Clear your client's aura and any blocked energy you find in his system. This step is crucial, because you want there to be clear pathways for the healing crystal and reiki energy to flow freely through the system.

4. Do your reiki hand protocols.

5. At the end of the session, remove your crystals from the crown down so that your client stays grounded, and any physical healing protocols you've used last.

6. Do a final quick clearing of his aura to remove any remaining or lingering debris released during the session.

7. Draw a raku at your client's feet to ground the healing energy, and then another between you to sever the psychic connection. If you haven't been attuned to the raku symbol, you can leave pieces of smoky quartz or hematite at his feet, and pass your selenite wand between yourself and your client to sever the connection.

8. Wash your hands, drink some water, and then offer your client some water. At this time you can choose to discuss what came up, if anything, during the session, and check to see how your client is feeling. Remember to always ask your client for permission first before offering any feedback, suggestions, or intuitive insight.

9. Do a quick energy clearing of your space and your own aura. If you've been paid in cash, you can give that a quick energy clearing, too, and then clear the crystals used in the session.

10. Either get ready for your next client or pack up for the day. Job well done!

As a final note, I've always encouraged clients to take it easy, avoid heavy food, vigorous exercise, or alcohol for at least one hour after their session so that the energy work can settle in their system. The same advice applies to healers, too, as your own energy will have been exposed to and potentially influenced by the crystals and reiki during the session.

Also, even though the healing energy flowing in the room came from Source, not you, it's still physically tiring to do healing work, especially if you're booked back to back all day. Part 4 of this book addresses a healer's self-care and offers some restorative practices you can try at the end of your healing day.

BASIC CHAKRA LAYOUT CHART

If you suspect a chakra is deficient or excessive, place the suggested crystal. If you're not sure or if you think the chakra's okay, then place the neutral crystal as suggested.

*Because rose quartz is essential love energy in a crystal, it can be used to help increase the flow of chi through a deficient heart chakra, as well as maintain a healthy flow.

†As an excessive crown chakra displays similar symptoms to a deficient root chakra, you can use smoky quartz at the crown to help ground some of the excessive energy in the body.

Basic Chakra Layout Chart

CHAKRA	DEFICIENT	NEUTRAL	EXCESSIVE
ROOT	Smoky Quartz	Ruby	Apache Tear
SACRAL	Carnelian	Orange Calcite or Fire Opal	Bloodstone
SOLAR PLEXUS	Citrine	Tiger Eye	Yellow Jasper or Honey Calcite
HEART	Watermelon Tourmaline or Rose Quartz	*Rose Quartz	Green Aventurine
THROAT	Amazonite	Blue Calcite	Blue Kyanite
THIRD EYE	Amethyst	Lapis Lazuli	Azurite
CROWN	Selenite	Moonstone	Smoky or †Smoky Elestial Quartz

Part 4

SELF-CARE
FOR THE HEALER

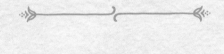

TAKING CARE OF YOURSELF

The most important lesson I've learned as a healer is how to take care of myself. It's been my experience that many healers tend to put everyone else's needs first, Taking care of clients, business, family, friends, even strangers requires a lot of our time and energy, and it gets to be exhausting. Healers are givers; we're wired to try to help people and make the world a better place, and learning how to balance that with our own self-care and needs is a lesson many of us have to learn. Self-care is essential: Your own health, happiness, and overall well-being are the foundation upon which everything is built. A strong foundation supports a happy spirit, a fulfilled life, a thriving business, a healthy body, personal joy, and professional achievement. A weak foundation leads to problems, obstacles, and discontent in all those areas, so no matter how much you work or how hard you try, it always feels as if the odds are stacked against you. That certainly was my experience.

I'm going to out myself here: I was the absolute worst at taking care of myself for a long time; my needs always came last. I put my work, my clients, and my calling first. I was completely absorbed in developing my craft, becoming the best healer I could be, and building a successful business. As a spiritual healer, you're essentially a small businessperson, so on top of all the spiritual work I was doing, I was responsible for my own marketing, bookkeeping, scheduling, and business management. It was a lot, and I was going from morning to night seven days a week. I rarely saw my friends, would gobble down food when I could, slept fitfully, and never, ever took a vacation.

I was often stressed, tired, and felt overworked and underserved, even though my business was doing well and people around me saw me as a success. I never felt like a success. I always felt like I was struggling, that I was never good enough, and my response to all that was to keep working harder and harder, more and more, until I was achieving my goals. I would wonder why I wasn't feeling 100 percent happy, even though I was living my dream.

My only real sanctuary at the time was my healing space and energy work. I'd step into my room, close the door, and leave it all on the other side. In my healing space I could breathe, let everything go, and settle into my zone, where the vibes could flow and my only focus was the work. I was a different person in that space: grounded, empowered, attuned to Spirit, at one with my crystals. I loved the feeling as the reiki flowed through me and I could tune into my client's energy. I always had a feeling of warmth, peace, and rightness. In those moments, I never questioned my choices or my path: I knew I was right where I was meant to be.

But the second I left my room, there, lurking in the hallway, was the feeling I'd left behind: that I was being of service to others but not to myself. That feeling would lumber home with me, and I would find myself questioning my choices, feeling fearful or resentful, and wondering how I could turn things around.

I had so much to be grateful for, and I truly was grateful! I was doing work I loved for a living, and I had so many wonderful clients and students, loving friends, and family. A roof over my head, clothes on my back, food to eat. But without adequate self-care, which for me included things like downtime, having fun, eating a healthy, balanced diet, and pursuing some *personal* dreams as well as professional goals, there was a part of me that felt neglected, starved, and unhappy.

Like athletes and performers, healers have needs that are unique to their skill set and vocation. My energy, thoughts, emotions, and physical health all directly impact my work and business. If I'm feeling down, I'm in a negative headspace, or if my energy's dark, my clients and students can sense it. The healing work won't be as strong, my intuition won't be as accurate, and if I'm sick I have to cancel (and healers don't get sick pay!). The energy of my business mirrors my own: If I'm in a low place, my business sinks there, too. I get cancellations, enrollment slows, sales drop. My own vibrations are entrained with those of my business, because I *am* my business.

It took me a little while to figure all this out, but once I realized that my own self-care and feelings of joy were the essential, magical ingredients that made everything better in my life, I began putting practices and boundaries in place to honor them. I still have good days and bad, but the benefits of self-care and making choices based on my happiness demonstrate themselves time and again. Whenever I'm taking care of myself, everything flourishes. Whenever I make choices based on my own happiness, and pursue dreams that come from my heart, I succeed. Do I ever make mistakes? Sure. Do I ever fail? Of course. That's how I learn. But I always feel in alignment with my truth, my purpose, and my soul. And so I'm grateful for the lessons.

No lesson has been as hard-won for me as the importance of self-care. While everybody's needs will differ based on their circumstances, I'm offering some suggestions to help you develop your own self-care practices based on what I found was essential for myself as a professional Crystal Reiki healer. Many training programs tend to not include teachings on self-care for healers. Apart from remembering that you are your own business, I think it's also valuable to note that healers *deserve* to be well-cared for.

We're in a world where the mainstream hasn't yet fully recognized our value, and yet more and more of us are answering the call and becoming healers because the world needs us. Increasing numbers of people are turning to us for help because they're not finding what they need elsewhere, and we're providing a beautiful and vital service.

It's time to eschew the belief that as healers we're meant to be selfless, impoverished, and embodiments of abnegation. As we heal, prosper, and grow stronger, so does the world around us. Take care of yourself first, and then you can take care of the rest.

SELF-CARE PRACTICES

I heard this bit of guidance passed on from one highly successful woman to another: "When you feel like you've got enough help, get yourself more." The more care and support you give, the more you're going to need to receive. This is how you keep your energy balanced and your well from running dry. A mentor of mine consistently advised me to only ever give from my surplus, which was wonderful guidance, but I had to figure out how to create that surplus from which to give!

Everything I suggest below I consider to be self-care essentials for a healer, but it is by no means meant to be an exhaustive list. Start here with what you feel you can make work for yourself, and then take a little time to reflect on what else you can add to your days or weeks that can be nourishing and supportive for you. Let your abundance mind-set expand here. Abundance begets abundance: The more you give to yourself, the better you feel; the better you feel, the better things become. This is an intrinsic part of your healing path and process.

Crystal Self-Healing

One of the most gorgeous and wonderful benefits of being a Crystal Reiki healer is that you can easily give yourself healing sessions. You've got all the tools, and as long as you've got someplace comfortable and quiet to lie down for a while, all you need is time.

For your own personal healing process, use any of the crystal healing protocols and layouts in this book. Be sure to follow your standard preparation steps and don't skimp on them! Do for yourself as you would do for others. When I do a crystal healing layout for myself, I go through all the prep and then I select my crystals. I place them all on a tray in the layout order that I'll be placing on them on my body, and then I set the tray where I can easily reach it after I'm lying down. I place the crystals on myself one by one, cover myself with a blanket, set the timer, and float away.

The following is a crystal healing layout I designed specifically to help restore and balance my energy at the end of a long week of client appointments. It helps to replenish vital resources and nourish chakras that are most used or drained during a week of healing sessions. The goals here are grounding, replenishing of vital chi and energy, chakra balancing, relieving stress, strengthening intuition and restoring the energy of the third eye chakra, clearing the crown chakra, raising frequency, and filling the system with soothing love and light. All in approximately 45 minutes. Not bad, right?

If you've been taught a reiki self-healing protocol, by all means use that in your session, or simply place your hands wherever you feel intuitively guided. Personally, I like to take a total load off and let the crystals do all the work. Do whatever feels best to you.

Weekly Restorative Layout for Crystal Reiki Healers

Duration: 25–45 minutes

Root: Smoky Quartz, Bloodstone, and Ruby

Sacral: Orange Calcite and Carnelian

Solar plexus: Honey Calcite, Jet, and Aragonite Star Cluster

Heart: Green Aventurine, Rose Quartz, and Rhodonite

Throat: Blue Calcite

Third Eye: Azurite

Crown: Selenite and Moonstone

Hands (option #1 for if you feel you need added energy clearing): Selenite in your receptive hand, Black Tourmaline in your dominant hand

Hands (option #2 for if you feel you need an added energy boost): Shiva Lingam in your receptive hand, Hematite in your dominant hand

Once your timer goes off, remove your crystals from the crown down so that you remain grounded, and then take it easy for the next hour or so and let the energy settle. So no exercise, heavy meals, alcohol, or loud music for at least an hour after your session. And don't forget to clear your crystals before you use them again!

Wearing Crystal Combinations

Crystal Reiki is a part of my daily life. I tune into my reiki and let the energy flow as I do gentle yoga poses first thing in the morning. I wear crystals all day, and I sleep with them at night, and most nights I'll prop my legs up for a bit and do some self-reiki in bed before falling asleep. These aren't things that take a lot of time, but they make a big difference for me in terms of supporting my daily needs and care. Depending on what energy I need, crystal vibes are always flowing through my system, and the reiki energy helps to reduce my feelings of stress and anxiety on a daily basis. I feel more self-love and self-worth as a result.

GROUNDING	PROTECTION	LOVE & COMPASSION	INTUITION	REIKI AMPLIFYING
Bloodstone	Black Tourmaline	Chrysocolla	Amethyst	Apophyllite
Ruby	Blue Kyanite	Cobalto Calcite	Merlinite	Danburite
Shiva Lingam	Jet	Rose Quartz	Moldavite	Mangano Calcite
Smoky Quartz	Labradorite	Watermelon Tourmaline	Moonstone	Quartz

Here are a few crystal protocols that I feel are unique to an energy healer's needs, supporting you in your daily life and work. You can wear crystals on a daily basis by placing them in your pockets, in pieces of jewelry, in a medicine bag that you wear or carry, or in a pouch that you can pop in your bra. Always be sure to clear any crystals worn daily on a nightly basis so that you keep their energy pure and strong.

Emotional calm and centering combination: You're human and there are days when you're going to feel angry, stressed, anxious, or upset; get in a conflict; or receive some disappointing news. And yet you still need to pull yourself together and get ready for a healing session. Going through your prep, as outlined in Part 2, will definitely help you, but you can also wear this combination for extra help: mangano calcite or cobalto calcite for compassion and acceptance of what you're feeling; smoky quartz to ground you and relieve stress; blue lace agate to calm and center your emotional self; and moonstone to reconnect to nurturing and soothing higher energy.

For empathic healers: Empaths require an extra level of care, as they're more susceptible to taking on their clients' energy. If you're an empath, I recommend always wearing jet during your sessions, as it absorbs energy in your stead. You may have to give it a quick clearing in between clients, depending on how well you've learned to shield yourself.

If you're a projecting empath and you're worried about your energy negatively impacting your client in some way, wear the Emotional calm and centering combination and add snowflake obsidian to it. This will help to neutralize any potentially unbalancing emotional energy coming from you, as well as helping you to project a healing, loving, and light-filled presence.

Energy-boosting combination: On days where I hadn't had enough sleep or I had a long day of sessions booked, I would rely on the following combination to keep my energy high and strong. It has the added benefits of grounding, stamina, increasing intuition, and raising your frequency so you can channel strong reiki energy even if your own energy feels low: shiva lingam, gold rutilated quartz, citrine, and red jasper.

Focused mind combination: You may have things on your mind, but when your session begins it's time for you to be focused on your client. Again, going through your prep, as outlined in Part 2, will help you, but we all have those moments where our minds just keep wandering or won't let something go. You can grab hold of the following crystal combination to help you get your mind-set back in the zone: blue fluorite or sapphire for focus, hematite or onyx for grounding, and morganite for self-forgiveness.

Psychic shield combination: You can wear the following combination to shield yourself from picking up harmful energy or psychic debris during a session. It's best to wear this over or as near to the heart chakra as you can: black tourmaline, black obsidian, fluorite, blue kyanite, and labradorite.

Healing session support combination: When I'm giving a healing session I always wear one crystal for grounding, one for protection, one for love and compassion, one for intuition and higher guidance, and one to amplify my reiki vibes. This covers all my main needs of support while I'm working, and helps me to be 100 percent of service to my client without worrying about taking any of his energy on. Below I've listed crystal suggestions for each category. Choose which one you feel most guided to (or an alternative if it's not listed), and build your own combo.

Food and Water

Obviously, I can't tell you how to eat, but your body can. If you feel fit, healthy, and nourished, then how you're eating is likely working for you. But if you don't, I highly recommend that you keep a food diary for a while. Record what you eat and how you feel afterward, not just physically, but also emotionally, mentally, and spiritually. Food affects every level of our well-being, and, as we're all different, different foods can affect us in different ways.

I've learned not to consume a lot of dairy the night before healing work because I found it had a tendency to block my crown chakra. I avoid sugar when I'm feeling wired yet tired because I've found it exacerbates the symptoms, and I also avoid it if I feel I need extra energy shielding because it seems to weaken my aura defenses. My intuition is stronger and my clairvoyance more defined when I go meat-free, and my claircognizance and gift for prophecy are far more accurate when I consume a plant-based, low-fat diet. Now that's me. Whether or not that's true for you depends on your body and its chemical reaction to certain foods. This is how the food journal comes in handy—you can let your body teach you how and how not to eat, and even when or when not to eat, based on your reactions to certain foods.

While channeling reiki is considered to be as healing for the healer as the person receiving it, being an energy healer still takes its toll on the body. As you're working, you're in a heightened state of frequency, electricity, and receptivity, and maintaining this state for an hour or more can be draining to your system. I used to fast during long healing days or when teaching reiki classes, and I was always a zombie by the end of the day. I now look back on that and shake my head. I finally learned to eat smaller, nourishing meals to help sustain me throughout the day and pack plenty of healthy snacks, water, and coconut water to help replenish my electrolytes. Getting in your daily vitamins, minerals, and nutritional requirements, as well as staying well-hydrated, are key to keeping you at the top of your game and avoiding burnout.

Always make sure you have access to clean, fresh drinking water during your sessions, and drink water whenever you feel the need to. I was taught in my reiki training to never remove my hands from my client until the end of the session; otherwise, I'd be breaking the connection and disrupting the flow. This has not been the truth of my experience. If I needed to grab a drink of water, adjust the volume on the music I was playing, or do whatever else, I just did it and then took a moment to reconnect to my reiki before coming back to my client. It was fine, and 99 percent of the time my clients never even noticed.

While I emphasize over and over again in this book that your focus should always be on your client during a session, this does not mean that you can't honor your own needs as well. You're the healer—you've got to be in a fit state to heal, so if that means you need to drink water during a session, drink water. Be sure to schedule in mealtimes and breaks (even if you're paying for an hourly rental). You deserve to be well-cared for and your needs have to be met. It's that simple.

Salt Baths

There's one self-care practice I have recommended to clients and students over and over again—taking salt baths. A warm, salty bath delivers a thorough aura clearing (make sure to dunk your head under a few times!), draws physical and energetic toxins from the body, and, depending on the type of salt you use (like Dead Sea, Himalayan, or Epsom), helps to replenish vital minerals in the body. As I mentioned above, we can become depleted in vital minerals and energy when doing healing work, so a nice salt bath once or twice a week can really help. The magnesium in an Epsom salt bath can also help to improve your sleep at night and ease achy or tired muscles. And, of course, there's the added bonus of being able to relax and unwind for 15 to 30 minutes!

Important things to note with salt baths: The water needs to be salty, so make sure you add anywhere from two to four cups of salt to your bathwater. You can find different salts at bulk prices online so that this doesn't cost you a huge amount of money. Also make sure that the water is warm enough that the salts dissolve, and that you have a glass of water before your bath so it doesn't dehydrate you. Finally, take a quick shower after your bath to rinse the salt off your skin and out of your hair. You can always shampoo at this point if you wish.

Some people opt out of bathing because it takes too much time. I get it—life is busy! But remember that the better you take care of yourself, the more your life can improve. Those 30 minutes a week could pay great dividends! If you don't have a bathtub, try the scrub I suggest below.

Baking Soda Shower Scrub

Not into taking baths or don't have a tub? Using a baking soda scrub in the shower is a fine alternative. Make sure you spread the baking soda all over your body, from head to toe, to help clear your aura. You can really feel the difference after a baking soda scrub, like you're extra sparkly and clean! It can double as a soap and a shampoo for those who wish it, and you can blend it into your shower gel or make a do-it-yourself scrub with coconut oil or honey as a base. I share some of my DIY aura-clearing recipes on my blog; you can go to my website, krista-mitchell.com and try my "Divine DIY Aura Scrub" if you're searching for some ideas.

Sleep

Most people need a $7\frac{1}{2}$–9-hour sleep cycle on a daily basis. There are plenty of resources online to help you learn more about sleep and how to improve its quality, so I'll stick to some spiritually related recommendations that could be of service to you.

Clear your energy every night before sleeping. If you have psychic debris hanging around in your aura all night, that can definitely affect your sleep. It can increase feelings of anxiety, disturbance, worry, fear, or lead to having uneasy dreams. Even if you sleep through the night, you can still wake up feeling tired in the morning. I make it a practice to clear my aura every night before crawling into bed, and it makes a huge difference, I've gone from waking periodically in the night to sleeping right through.

Clear the energy of your bedroom regularly. Any time I tussle with what feels like a dark spirit in my dreams at night, or if I feel a weird energy presence when I'm trying to fall asleep, that's a sign that it's time to clear my space. You can follow the same steps for space clearing outlined in Part 2 for your bedroom, and I recommend doing that on a regular basis so that it never becomes a problem. How regular depends on what feels best to you; I'm in the habit of clearing mine on a weekly basis.

Diffuse a banishing or protective essential oil. Palo santo, frankincense, lavender, rose, or bergamot are all good choices that will also have a soothing effect on your mood.

Light a Himalayan salt lamp. Light has been used since the beginning of time for protection and to help banish darkness, and the ionizing effects of the warmed salt help to balance the energy in your space.

Meditate for 5 to 10 minutes while holding rose quartz. Rose quartz emits soothing, warm, loving energy that helps to bring ease to your system, while the meditation helps to calm and center the mind.

Sleep with lepidolite, selenite, or moonstone under your pillow. These crystals have peaceful, serene, and sleepy vibes that help you drift off at night. If your sleep pattern has been changed, disrupted, or if you're suffering from jet lag, fall asleep while holding or wearing mookaite jasper. It helps you to settle back into a natural rhythm.

Staying Committed to Your Own Healing Process

I've mentioned shadow self-healing a fair bit in this book in relation to your clients, but that work applies to yourself, too. We all have shadows, we all have wounds, limiting beliefs, things we're resisting or denying, excuses we make, fears, shames, and regrets. The more you work through your own stuff, the more empowered, whole, and self-actualized you become. And, as a healer, the more you're able to help others through the same process (or at least understand where they're coming from). As a healer you need to always be working on yourself to authentically embody the work you do.

Another recommendation is to receive healing work from somebody else. We all need to support each other. The benefit of seeing another healer on at least a monthly basis is that you get to be the *client* for a change! Get an energy tune-up and a thorough aura clearing. Don't try to be it all—it's so healing and nourishing to receive.

Continuing Education

Last, but not least, it's so good for the soul to keep learning and for you to keep making that investment in yourself. As a healer, your life is your school, and teachers will present themselves to you in all forms: your clients, students, kids, parents, friends, rivals, enemies, loves, and heartbreakers. Your crystals, clients, experience, and your own healing process will teach you an enormous amount, and present countless opportunities for you to develop and evolve. Beyond that, there's always more to learn! Keep reading, take classes, and seek out mentors and guides to help you. Be brave, open, and curious. Take what resonates as truth to your heart and leave the rest.

You're on the most wondrous path as a healer and as a spiritual being, and it can lead to the most magical and fulfilling existence. Invest in yourself; invest in your work and your own healing process; grow, dream, and realize your truth. I feel truly blessed to be walking this path with you!

— *Krista*

Energy Clearing	Citronella
	Coconut
	Copaiba
	Copal
	Dragon's Blood
	Frankincense
	Lavender
	Lemon
	Lemongrass
	Mint
	Myrrh
	Palo Santo
	Rue
	Sandalwood
	White Sage

TABLES OF CORRESPONDENCES
CRYSTALS

Energy Clearing	
	Aegirine
	Ajoite
	Black Tourmaline
	Blue Tourmaline
	Calcite (any color, but for this purpose clear works best)
	Elestial Quartz
	Jet
	Moldavite
	Smoky Quartz
	Sugilite
	Tourmaline Quartz
Grounding	
	Bloodstone
	Boji stones
	Hematite
	Nuumite
	Red Calcite
	Red Jasper
	Ruby
	Shiva Lingam
	Smoky Quartz or Smoky Citrine
	Tiger's Eye or Tiger Iron

TABLES OF CORRESPONDENCES
CRYSTALS

Energy Sheilding and Protection	Apache Tear
	Blue Kyanite
	Black Obsidian
	Black Tourmaline
	Fluorite
	Infinite
	Jet
	Labradorite
	Salt Staurolite
	Spirit Quartz
Grounding (Soul-Centered Focus)	Apophyllite
	Larimar
	Nuumite
	Sodalite

CRYSTAL KEY ○ Stones Used in Case Studies

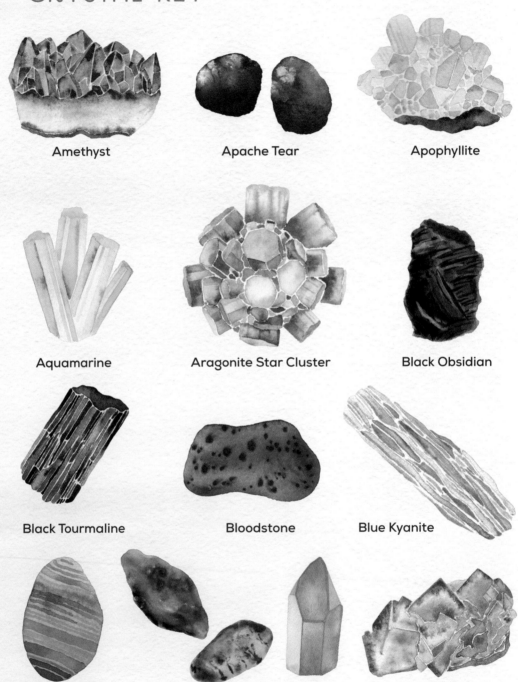

Amethyst

Apache Tear

Apophyllite

Aquamarine

Aragonite Star Cluster

Black Obsidian

Black Tourmaline

Bloodstone

Blue Kyanite

Carnelian

Chrysocolla

Citrine

Fluorite

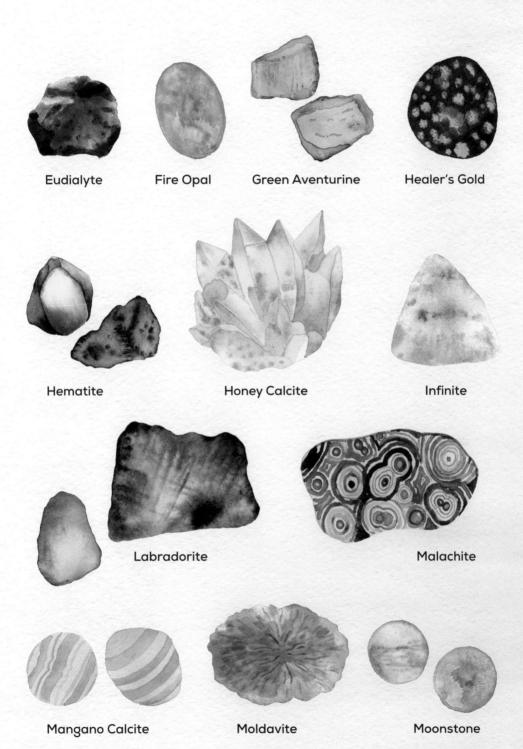

Eudialyte

Fire Opal

Green Aventurine

Healer's Gold

Hematite

Honey Calcite

Infinite

Labradorite

Malachite

Mangano Calcite

Moldavite

Moonstone

Pink Kunzite

Quartz Point

Rhodochrosite

Rhodonite

Rose Quartz

Ruby

Sapphire

Scolecite

Selenite

Smoky Elestial Quartz

Smoky Quartz

Snowflake Obsidian

Sodalite

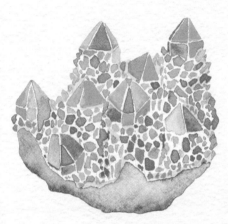

Spirit Quart

Sugilite

Sunstone

Tiger Eye

Tourmaline Quartz

CRYSTAL HEALING PROPERTIES

Physical healing properties of the listed crystals

Agate, fire: Increases levels of testosterone in the system.

Amethyst: Reduces physical and emotional levels of stress in the body.

Apache tear (translucent black obsidian): Helps the body settle into stillness and relax; reduces/balances excessive energy in the root chakra that can lead to imbalances in the parasympathetic nervous system.

Apatite, blue: Helps to reduce the appetite and channels that energy back into the body for use in physical activity or pursuits.

Aquamarine: Reduces inflammation; cools and soothes irritated tissues.

Aventurine, green: Increases metabolic rate and flow of vitality and healing chi throughout the body; helps to support optimal O_2/CO_2 exchange.

Azurite: Reduces inflammation, accelerates the body's natural healing process, brings ease to areas of physical tension.

Bloodstone: Accelerates healing; especially potent for blood, tissue, inflammatory conditions, skin, and bone-related health issues.

Blue jade: Relaxes the bronchial muscles; improves congestive issues.

Boji stone: Draws Earth energy up through the body, rapidly increasing levels of chi and vitality.

Calcite, blue: Reduces inflammation; soothes irritated tissues.

Calcite, green: Gently buffers and dissolves energy blockages and congestion, creating freer flow of healing chi throughout the body; increases natural levels of vitality and blood circulation.

Calcite, honey: Relaxes and brings ease to inflamed or irritated tissues; helps to maintain neutral pH and temperatures in the body.

Calcite, red: Gently buffers and dissolves energy blockages in the root chakra, freeing up more flow of healing chi and fluids throughout the body; helps to purify the lymphatic system and draw toxins out of the blood.

Carnelian: Stimulates the reproductive system and the instinct to reproduce; increases physical sensations of pleasure and desire; improves blood circulation in the lower half of the body.

Celestite: Reduces inflammation; accelerates healing.

Charoite: Gently clears and detoxifies impurities stored in the blood and tissues; nurtures the cells with vital, supportive chi.

Chrysocolla: Cools and soothes; gently restores balance and energy.

Citrine: Energizes, fortifies, and nourishes the lymphatic system, increasing lymphatic function and flow of fluids; improves overall digestion; stimulates the immune system.

Copper: Increases flow of healing chi; accelerates healing; helps to fight viruses, fungus, and unhealthy bacteria.

Dravite (brown tourmaline): Helps to detoxify, purge wastes, and soothe inflammation in the digestive system, improving overall function.

Emerald: Improves circulation, supports homeostasis, accelerates healing.

Epidote: Draws to the surface what needs to be released in order to effect deep healing.

Fluorite: Supports optimal cognitive and physical brain function.

Galena: Draws impurities out of the body and supports the natural detoxification and elimination process.

Healer's gold: Draws powerful levels of healing chi and energy to the body.

Hematite: Increases the healing flow of blood and chi; accelerates the repair of body tissues; relieves pain.

Jasper, mookaite: Helps the system come back into alignment or balance with its own circadian rhythm and sleep/wake homeostasis, and supports healthy levels of melatonin and cortisol in the body.

Jasper, ocean: Relieves tension and brings ease to overactive or overheated areas of the body.

Jasper, red: Increases the body's physical stamina; accelerates and supports the healing and repair of tissues, cartilage, and bone.

Jet: Absorbs stress and lower/harmful frequencies.

Kyanite, blue: Supports optimal func-tion of the tonsils and lymphatic system; reduces inflammation; and increases healing flow of chi in the throat, ears, and nose.

Lepidolite: Its frequencies signal to the hypothalamus and the body's internal clock that it is time for sleep.

Malachite: Accelerates the body's natural healing and recovery process.

Pyrite: Increases flow of blood, bodily fluids, and energy to areas of the body; stimulates the sympathetic nervous system and primal urges and instincts.

Quartz, gold rutilated: Fortifies, strengthens, and energizes the kidneys and kidney tissue.

Quartz, rose: Soothes the body's emotional response to stress and tension.

Quartz, smoky elestial: Draws powerful light energy into the body that purges and releases toxins, impurities, viruses, and negative or harmful energy that has manifested or been stored in the body.

Ruby: Stimulates the root chakra, increasing flow of energy, vitality, and healing chi throughout the body; increases physical sensations of pleasure and sense of fulfillment.

Selenite: Reduces pain and inflammation, dissolves blocked energy, rapidly increases flow of light energy from Source into the body.

Shiva lingam: Rapidly increases flow of chi and Earth energy throughout the body; helps to restore hormonal balance; stimulates the reproductive system; increases sperm count.

Sugilite: Draws healing life force energy down into the body from Source; accelerates deep healing and transformation.

Tiger iron: Combines the healing energy of hematite, red jasper, and tiger's eye; fortifies and strengthens all parts of the body.

Tiger's eye: Gentle energizer that helps to restore natural function and homeostasis to the body.

Tourmaline, black: Neutralizes energy imbalances; reduces pain.

Tourmaline, green: Supports and encourages accelerated and efficient healing at a cellular level; channels healing chi and additional energy to any part of the body.

Tourmaline, red: Increases blood flow and metabolic rate; dilates blood vessels and capillaries; supports cellular function and repair.

Unakite: Aligns the physical and emotional healing energies and will of the body in pursuit of deep healing and overall wellness.

Mental and emotional healing properties of the listed crystals:

Amazonite: Strengthens the connection between the heart and the throat chakra, so that it's easier to tune into our feelings and our authentic self, and be willing to own and express our truth.

Amethyst: Calms anxiety, soothes anger, and shields against negativity, including that of our own inner self, feelings, tendencies, and thoughts. Creates space in the mind for consideration and contemplation, so that we can respond, rather than simply reacting on impulse.

Ametrine: Combines the individual healing properties of both amethyst and citrine, and also helps to strengthen the connection between the third eye chakra and the solar plexus, improving alignment and communication between the intuition and the will.

Angelite: Helps to slow the pace of thoughts in the mind, creating a greater sense of calm and quiet. Soothes feelings of burnout and significantly reduces anxiety.

Apache tear: Offers gentle ease and healing from grief, allowing us to become aware of the source of our pain and upset without necessarily bringing those feelings up to the surface. Provides the healing energy we need to begin to move through grief, recover from loss, and let go of past wounding.

Apatite, golden: A crystal of will, manifestation, and inner fire. Bolsters low self-esteem, increases a sense of personal strength and boundaries, and helps us to develop a more defined sense of who we are in the world and what we want to contribute to it.

Apophyllite: Encourages detachment from the ego and strengthens the connection to our higher self and wisdom, allowing us to view things from a higher, less fear-based perspective.

Aquamarine: Bolsters our sense of courage while calming and soothing feelings of fear, anxiety, apprehension, and emotional overwhelm.

Aragonite star cluster: Instills feelings of empowerment, leadership, kindness, and generosity, and supports the emotional body in healing deep wounds that are still fresh and painful. Increases feelings of self-confidence, self-sufficiency, and the innate belief that this too shall pass. Supports us in being willing to heal and move forward in a positive fashion.

Aventurine, green: Replenishes depleted heart chakra energy, so that we are better able to balance what we give and put out into the world, and what we are willing to receive. Increases feelings of worthiness, deserving, and commitment to our own needs, boundaries, and self-care.

Azurite: Widens a narrowed perspective so that we are more open and receptive to ideas, guidance, and inspiration, and are able to come at things from different angles and think about things in different ways than we're accustomed to doing.

Bloodstone: Helps us to feel more grounded, stable, and secure within ourselves. Creates a feeling of having a solid inner foundation from which we can build relationships and form healthy emotional connections with the outside world.

Blue lace agate: Calms, collects, and focuses our mental and emotional energy, so that we can pursue and complete tasks, set goals, and follow through on intentions without being distracted or consumed by our emotions.

Blue sapphire: Sharpens the mind and our sense of clarity and focus so that we can perform tasks and work through obligations with greater organization, productivity, and mental acuity. Reduces feelings of mental and emotional overwhelm so that we can remain present for the tasks at hand.

Calcite, blue: Reduces feelings of fear, lack, anxiety, and apprehension. Calms and centers the emotional body and eases feelings of nervousness or trepidation.

Calcite, honey: Creates feelings of self-assuredness and stability in the solar plexus chakra, which can help us navigate and negotiate turbulent changes, transitions, upheaval, or reorientation with greater confidence and ease.

Calcite, mangano: Supports us in experiencing more authentic acceptance, compassion, gratitude, and forgiveness, both for ourselves and others. Helps to gently clear feelings of heaviness or blockage in the heart chakra.

Calcite, optical: Helps us to see things from a different perspective and to change conditioned patterns of thought, behavior, and assumption.

Calcite, orange: Gently clears and restores balance to the sacral chakra, increasing the healing flow of chi and improving our sense of possibility, levels of passion, creativity, optimism, and willingness to engage with the outside world.

Carnelian: Immediately begins to restore and increase the flow of chi through the sacral chakra, energizing feelings of passion, sensuality, sexuality, vigor, zest for life, and emotional strength. Helps to ground us in our own personal power, sense of identity, and ability to take action, dramatically improving our feelings of personal power and sovereignty.

Chrysocolla: A stone of gentle, mothering vibration that helps us to soften and both feel and express more compassion for ourself and others. It is a goddess stone that can increase feelings of kindness and femininity.

Chrysoprase: Helps loosen the grip of insecurity, angst, woe, and general unease in our system, so that we can focus on our own personal sources of fun, creativity, and joy. Increases feelings of altruism, confidence, creativity, and compassion.

Citrine: Boosts optimism, willingness to engage with the world, a "can-do" attitude, and imbues us with an overall sense of positivity, happiness, and confidence. Increases the flow of creative and artistic ideas, inspiration, and the energy to create.

Covelite: Brings our shadow-based beliefs, unhealthy commitments, fears, and other repressed feelings and thoughts up to the surface of our awareness so that we can begin to work through them and heal. It is especially beneficial if we feel consistently blocked, stuck, or unable to improve our circumstances or move forward. It helps us to reclaim our personal power and the potential that we've either discounted or did not believe was possible for us. The energy of covelite is intense and direct in its action, so we need to be ready and willing to go through the process if we work with this stone.

Eudialyte: Helps ground the energy of our heart chakra in our root chakra, supporting and guiding us in following our heart's desires and our soul purpose in our daily, physical life. Helps us to live from a more heart-centered place, and to build both a professional and a personal life that is more joyful and fulfilling.

Fire agate: Emits frequencies of yang, or masculine sensuality, sexuality, creativity, virility, and passionate expression. Increases feelings of overall satisfaction, security, plenty, and fulfillment.

Fluorite (multi-color): Activates, strengthens, and supports mental function, acuity, ability to learn and remember, and logical and linear thinking; increases levels of aptitude and intelligence, and clarity of thought, focus, and purpose.

Fluorite (predominantly green): Helps to bring focus, awareness, and clarity of purpose, action, and feelings to the heart chakra. Beneficial for those of us who want to genuinely pursue deeper levels of self-awareness and self-acceptance.

Fluorite (predominantly yellow): Helps strengthen the connection between the third eye chakra and the solar plexus chakra, which increases levels of communication and intuitive understanding, and helps to align the intuition with the will so that it is easier to follow our intuitive guidance. Also attunes our intuitive guidance to function in support of our intentions.

Garnet (almandine): Increases feelings of passion, sensuality, sexuality, aesthetics, appreciation, abundance, and zeal.

Hematite: Helps to ground and anchor us in our decisions, commitments, and goals, and energizes our feelings and ability to take action in pursuit of them. Provides the stamina and emotional strength to bravely face and address what needs to be healed and changed; to assert our boundaries, feel empowered, and hold our ground in conflict; and not to be swayed by our ego, self-sabotaging behaviors, or peer pressure.

Jasper, ocean: Creates an inner sense of ease, relaxation, and joy. Helps to reduce feelings of stress, worry, anxiety, or fearful anticipation. Wearing it helps us to embody more of a vacation mind-set or vibe.

Jasper, red: Boosts feelings of emotional stamina, stability, resilience, determination, courage, and perseverance.

Kunzite, pink: Emits the divine love ray that helps us to feel lighter, more joyful, loving, and emotionally at ease. Helps to comfort the child within as we engage in the healing process from childhood wounding, trauma, or pain.

Kyanite, blue: Streamlines mental energy and strengthens the connection between the third eye and throat chakras, supporting us in better articulating thoughts, expressing ideas, communicating feelings, debating or negotiating terms, and mediating between the needs of the heart and the edicts of the mind. Helps to empower our voice and confidence in speaking up and speaking out.

Malachite: Brings repressed emotions and emotional energy up to the surface so that it can be acknowledged, healed, and released. Helps us to reclaim a greater sense of self-confidence, self-awareness, self-worth, and personal power after having undergone deep emotional healing work, making it a stone of leadership and nobility. This is a powerful crystal that works quickly, so it needs to be handled judiciously.

Morganite: A crystal of infinite love, emotional healing, and warmth that helps us to feel more unconditionally loving toward ourself and others. Potent in grief healing and forgiveness work.

Obsidian, black: Helps to guide our awareness through shadow-self healing work, so that we can uncover the causes of what's blocking us, holding us back in life, or keeping us stuck in negative patterns, thoughts, beliefs, and choices.

Obsidian, snowflake: Grounds the light of our spirit and wisdom in our physical experience, which helps to emotionally support us through challenging, painful times. Helps us to feel less alone and more connected to and supported by something greater, the Universe, or the Divine.

Onyx: Grounds and centers our energy and attention, and increases our sense of will and determination, so that we can focus and streamline our actions, efforts, and choices in pursuit of our goals, while limiting any distractions or deterrents.

Peridot: A crystal of warmth, joy, love, abundance, and generosity that helps us choose happiness and passionately engage with the world.

Pyrite: Powerfully expands and increases the flow of chi through our solar plexus chakra, firing up our will, determination, ambition, desire for action, aggression, empowerment, and sense of worthiness and being deserving.

Quartz, blue: Stimulates and expands the throat chakra, improving our ability to create, manifest, and express ourselves both artistically and emotionally.

Quartz, clear: Magnifies and amplifies the energy of intent, and focuses and directs that energy. Must be used with intention.

Quartz, lithium: Rapidly expands the heart chakra, flooding the system with loving chi that quickly reduces or subdues feelings of anxiety, fear, stress, and worry in times of crisis.

Quartz, rose: Improves our overall feelings of self-love, self-worth, and self-acceptance. Healing for emotional wounds and insecurities, and supports us in taking more loving care of ourself and others. Increases feelings of compassion, love, generosity, warmth, and comfort in our own skin.

Quartz, smoky: Clears feelings of stress and negativity from the system, helps to ground and center our awareness in our present reality.

Quartz, smoky elestial: Supports deep mental and emotional healing by grounding light energy in the system, clearing feelings of negativity, self-loathing, stress, fear, hatred, and spite. Helps us cultivate a greater awareness of what's good in ourselves and in the world. Engenders feelings of light and hope, without denying the darkness.

Quartz, spirit: Helps us to feel greater levels of courage, strength, determination, and an unwillingness to be pulled into negative patterns of thought or frames of mind.

Rhodochrosite: Deeply healing for old or childhood trauma, violation, abuse, violence, and all other forms of deep wounding to the emotional self and psyche. Can be placed on the heart chakra or the solar plexus chakra to help facilitate the healing of dysmorphia, disassociation, or other forms of self-identity crisis. Is loving and gradual in its effects.

Rhodonite: Helps us to feel less vulnerable, more open, courageous, and willing to experience and share loving intimacy, and to engage in forming relationships (either platonic or romantic). Can be placed on the heart chakra when we are in the final stages of recovering from heartbreak, loss, or grief.

Rubellite (red tourmaline): Deep heart healing for those who are suffering from lifelong histories of self-abuse, loathing, and fear of being loved. It's a crystal that teaches us how to love again, first ourselves and then others. Helps to restore feelings of trust, faith, and belief in ourselves and others.

Ruby: Helps to expand and strengthen the root chakra, improving our ability to provide for ourselves, heal family and cultural relationships, and live our life in a way that feels in alignment with our values, beliefs, and desires. Increases feelings of self-sovereignty, authority, personal power, and leadership, as well as the ability to feel passionate, sensual, and emotionally available. It is a crystal of empowerment, creativity, and abundance that helps to improve our overall sense of well-being and fulfillment in life.

Scolecite: Harmonizes various frequencies of energy so that they are entrained and functioning toward a highest intent or highest good. Creates a sense of overall well-being, security, connection to our own wisdom and the Divine, so that we can make what we feel are wise choices and overcome obstacles and feelings of overwhelm or insignificance in life.

Selenite: Rapidly opens and expands the crown chakra, increasing the flow of light through the body, strengthening our connection to our higher self, wisdom, the Divine, and lifting our mind-set out of the humdrum of daily affairs, problems, and afflictions. Dramatically soothes or dissolves feelings of tension, stress, constraint, burden, or overwhelm. Helps us to feel more serene, calm, and peaceful overall.

Sodalite: Supports us in becoming more aware of who we are, our inner working, and thought processes, as well as discerning patterns of thinking or decision making that come from our fear-based or shadow self, as opposed to our wiser, more loving, and intuitive self. It helps us to see ourselves with greater clarity so that we can become aware of what needs to be healed and released, or what needs to be encouraged and cultivated. It also facilitates the learning and remembering of new information and skills, and the study of new modalities, languages, or philosophies.

Sugilite: Activates and accelerates deep mental and emotional healing by drawing greater amounts of divine light and love into wounded areas or areas of dysfunction. Sugilite works on the subconscious and is effective whether we're aware of the issue(s) it's healing or not.

Sunstone: A crystal of leadership, self-sovereignty, and confidence that helps us to firmly but compassionately assert our boundaries, needs, feelings, desires, and self. It is an especially potent crystal to work with if we're having trouble saying no when we need to, or if we struggle with honoring our priorities and putting ourselves first.

Tiger iron: Increases our sense of will, determination, self-protection, empowerment, courage, fortitude, and focus.

Tiger's eye: Promotes feelings of balance, emotional strength, stability, resilience, and empowerment.

Tourmaline, watermelon: Restorative and healing for people who feel closed off, timid, vulnerable, insensitive, or emotionally resistant. Gently and gradually opens the heart chakra so that we can feel a growing sense of love, openness, compassion, and warmth toward ourselves and others.

Unakite: Helps to bring our physical self, urgings, impulses, and cravings into greater alignment with our loving, heart-centered self. Supports us in our emotional healing and recovery from addictions, self-sabotaging behaviors, and mental conditioning brought on by the shadow self and early childhood trauma.

Vanadinite: Energizes and increases the flow of chi between the root, sacral, and solar plexus chakras, dramatically increasing our stamina, resilience, vitality and energy levels, and determination, to help us move undaunted through times of challenge, struggle, duress, obstacle, heavy workload, and seemingly insurmountable odds.

Spiritual healing properties of the listed crystals:

Agate, holly blue: Powerfully attunes our third eye chakras with the pineal gland, activating and strengthening our psychic abilities (clairvoyance, in particular) and connecting them to divine sources of light.

Agate, moss: Increases our sense of overall well-being, abundance, and fulfillment, and our awareness of the great abundance of the natural world, thereby attuning our frequencies to attracting more.

Ajoite: Channels high, divine frequencies of light energy and the divine feminine, helping us to integrate more of the healing power, wisdom, and spiritual awareness of our higher selves. Repels lower frequencies and negative spirits.

Amethyst: Increases flow of chi to the third eye chakra, which strengthens our ability to hear our intuition and receive higher guidance.

Angelite: Emits soothing, gentle yet high-frequency vibrations that help attract angelic helpers, guidance, and healing energy.

Apophyllite: Helps us detach from the lower, more worldly concerns of the ego so that we have greater access to the wisdom of our higher self, higher dimensions, or higher realms, including those of the ascended masters and angels, and the Akashic records. Amplifies healing energy through space and time.

Apophyllite, green: Helps us to become more aware of the consciousness and intelligence of nature and nature spirits, and tune in to the realm of the fae and the spirit of the Green Man. Channels the healing and restorative energy of natural places even while in urban spaces.

Astrophyllite: Helps us tap into our past-life and karmic history, spiritual DNA, and soul-level truth, so that we develop greater spiritual self-awareness and acceptance, and heal karmic wounds and beliefs.

Azurite: Restores an excessive third eye chakra by balancing and redistributing the flow of chi. Brings greater awareness and energy to our psychic abilities, particularly activating and strengthening the gifts of clairvoyance, clairaudience, and prophecy.

Blue apatite: In manifestation work, when we speak our desires out loud, we give them energy and power. Blue apatite magnifies and amplifies this power, accelerating the manifestation process.

Blue kyanite: Aligns the third eye with the throat chakra, strengthening our ability to conceive, clarify, and articulate ideas, information, wisdom, and knowledge. Balances the flow of chi through the throat chakra so that our communication is governed with greater consciousness. Heightens our awareness of our psychic abilities and intuition.

Calcite, blue: Clears energy blockages and increases the flow of chi through a deficient throat chakra, resulting in greater ease of communication.

Calcite, clear: Clears blockages in the third eye and crown chakras, and helps to regulate the flow of life force and light or divine energy entering the body through the crown chakra, so that the body can more easily ground and integrate the vibrations.

Calcite, green: Clears energy blockages in the heart chakra and restores vitality.

Calcite, honey: Relieves tension in the solar plexus chakra, especially when experiencing psychic attack. Helps to clear energy blockages in the solar plexus and increases the flow of chi.

Calcite, mangano: Helps us to be in a place of unconditional loving acceptance, so that healing energy, love, and light flow freely through and around us.

Calcite, optical: Shifts our perspective and helps us to see greater possibility in our lives, so that we are better able to work toward manifesting our visions and dreams, and less likely to be blocked by our own doubts or limiting beliefs.

Calcite, orange: Clears energy blockages in the sacral chakra and increases the creative flow of chi.

Calcite, red: Clears energy blockages in the root chakra and increases the healing flow of chi.

Carnelian: Increases the flow of chi and strengthens the function of the sacral chakra. Warrior goddess energy.

Cavansite: Activates and strengthens dormant clairaudient and clairvoyant abilities, and expands our consciousness so that we have greater access to higher and hidden realms.

Celestite: Raises our frequency and brings our awareness to our crown chakras and our divine connection to higher consciousness, beings, and realms. Helps us to access angelic frequencies and can attract angelic protection and intervention. Opens a gateway of energy and information between our soul and our higher self so that we can begin to comprehend and pursue our soul purpose and spiritual evolution in this lifetime.

Chalcopyrite: Channels and emits divine masculine frequencies, supporting us in pursuing our life purpose and taking greater action to achieve more mindful, conscious ideals.

Chiastolite: Helps attune your clairvoyant and clairaudient abilities to be able to see and hear nature spirits and fairies. Provides psychic protection against darker elemental spirits. Increases our ability to manifest ideas and desires on the earthly plane.

Chrysanthemum stone: Attracts good luck and abundance; expands our abundance consciousness and our feelings of worthiness and deserving. Helps to shift our mind-set from one of negative attraction to positive.

Chrysocolla: A goddess stone that channels loving, divine frequencies of gentleness, compassion, and healing. Helps us to intuit the deeper or hidden meaning in things. Expands the throat and third eye chakras.

Citrine: Energizes and supports the function of the solar plexus chakra. Heightens our natural clairsentient and intuitive abilities. Attracts prosperity and abundance.

Danburite: A crystal of higher consciousness and divine activation that rapidly raises our frequencies, supporting us in channeling messages and information from spirits and higher realms; facilitates access to the Akashic records and helps us glean meaning and additional information from spiritual texts. Lifts us powerfully out of a material world mind-set and into a state of divine awareness, bliss, and contemplation.

Emerald: Helps us to tap into the greater loving potential of our heart chakras, helping us to feel more genuine oneness, completeness, connection to the Divine, compassion, unconditional love, and forgiveness.

Epidote: Channels, attunes and directs more of our energy toward that which we are seeking to manifest, bringing our visions, plans, and desires into our physical reality more quickly. Can also draw on subconscious and shadow-based desires that we are not aware of, but that are working against us.

Eudialyte: Grounds our heart energy in our root chakra, facilitating and supporting us in pursuing our heart's dreams and our soul-based desires in our reality. Especially potent for people who are seeking to live more heart-centered, authentic, and empowered lives. It helps to align our energy with our goals, so that we are more likely to attract helpful people, opportunities, and other synchronistic events that will support us in achieving our dreams.

Fluorite: Has a shielding or cloaking effect on the aura, helping to protect us from various forms of psychic attack and malevolent intentions. Helps to enhance our dream states so that our experiences and memories are more vivid.

Garnet, green: Expands our feelings about and awareness of the great abundance of Source and nature that surround us. Opens our heart to be willing to receive and share more, so that we feel less limited and lack-based in our thinking, and more expansive in our sense of possibility and potential. Attunes our own frequencies to that of abundance, so that we attract more abundance.

Green aventurine: Balances the heart chakra and redistributes excessive energy, so that we are better able to see and feel how we are out of balance, and make healing choices accordingly. Increases our willingness to receive, thereby removing the blocks to abundance and prosperity that can be created by low self-worth and fear.

Healer's gold: Shields a healer's heart chakra during a healing session so that she is less likely to take on her client's energy during a session. Amplifies healing frequencies and expands the reiki channel through a healer for greater reiki flow.

Herkimer diamond: Stimulates the pineal gland and the third eye chakra, and activates dormant psychic abilities. Enhances the dream state and increases our ability to remember and interpret our dreams.

Infinite: Heightens and attunes our awareness to the nature and fae realms, particularly through clairsentience. Heals, restores, and strengthens a damaged aura.

Labradorite: Potently increases our ability to manifest and initiate powerful transformation, first within, then without. Provides powerful shielding for the heart chakra and both the emotional and spiritual fields of the aura. Heightens both intuitive and claircognizant abilities.

Lapis lazuli: Helps us to keep in tune with our inner and outer awareness, supports the balanced function of the third eye chakra, and increases our ability to think for ourselves while trusting our intuition.

Larimar: Helps us connect to our own divine feminine energies and wisdom, as well as channeling goddess energies.

Lemurian jade: Amplifies and empowers our manifestation abilities by enhancing our spiritual connection to the physical plane. That which we believe, we achieve.

Merlinite: Greatly enhances our psychic abilities, mediumship abilities, and connection to inner and outer magic.

Moldavite: Initiates and accelerates all forms of transformation, psychic and spiritual ability, and healing. Arguably the most high-frequency crystal found on the planet, it can be overwhelming for some, so always ask a client first before using it in healing work.

Moonstone: Gentle, yin, intuitive energy that connects us more powerfully with moon cycles, energy, and goddess affiliations. Helps maintain balance at the crown chakra.

Pink kunzite: Channels light rays of divine love, compassionate action, and the vibrations of joy and gratitude.

Pyrite: Stimulates the solar plexus chakra and supports us in manifesting greater levels of prosperity, achievement, and success on the material plane.

Quartz, angel aura: Uplifts and pacifies the spirit, and increases our ability to have faith and positive expectation.

Quartz, aqua aura: Helps us to tune out the inner voice of doubt and focus more acutely on our psychic abilities, especially clairaudience.

Quartz, clear: Amplifies, magnifies, and directs all frequencies of energy. Can enhance psychic and spiritual abilities when used with that intention.

Quartz, elestial: Draws greater amounts of life-force and divine-light energy into the body and physical plane, helping us to live a more spiritual experience in our daily lives. It also helps us to clear low frequencies and negativity from our aura, and to access the wisdom and energy we need to effect karmic healing. Also increases our connection to the angelic realm.

Quartz, gold rutilated: Strengthens our connection to the divine masculine; enhances our ability to communicate with spirits in the ascended master realm through prayer, telepathy, and meditation.

Quartz, rose: Helps us to heal the heart so that we can come into a more loving, accepting, and compassionate relationship with ourselves and others. Can help us to attract love, friendship, and good will into our lives.

Quartz, silver rutilated: Strengthens our connection to the divine feminine and goddess energy, particularly moon and water goddesses.

Quartz, smoky: Grounds energy in the body, increases our connection to Earth and Earth energy, and stimulates greater flow of chi through the root chakra.

Quartz, spirit: Attunes our psychic abilities to all forms of spirit realms, particularly those of ghosts and fae, so that we can see, hear, and feel them with greater accuracy.

Rhodonite: Links the heart chakra with the root chakra, so we feel more compelled and courageous in honoring and following our heart's guidance.

Rubellite: Helps us to tap into the wellspring of our soul's love, so that we can more fully honor and accept ourselves as divinely whole, yet imperfect, beings, and pursue our life or soul purpose. Energizes a deficient heart chakra and helps us to heal on a deep, spiritual level.

Ruby: Helps to maintain a balanced, healthy, and functional root chakra.

Scolecite: Harmonizes our divine masculine and feminine energies so that we can function from a place of spiritual balance within. Expands and strengthens the crown chakra, and helps us to come into greater alignment within in terms of our choice of belief systems and moral integrity.

Selenite: Opens, expands, and strengthens the crown chakra, increasing the flow of chi to our higher, spiritual selves and wisdom, facilitating communication with higher realms, including those of the angelic and Akashic. Quickly raises our frequency so that we are better able to perform healing, channeling, and mediumship work. Fills a space and our own bodies with greater amounts of light and divine energy.

Seraphinite: Opens our heart chakra's channel and connection to the angelic realm, so that we can feel angelic love and compassion, and receive healing energy from the angels. Also helps us experience an overall feeling of greater wholeness and serenity.

Shiva lingam: Dramatically increases the accuracy of our intuition, and our ability to honor and follow it in our daily lives.

Staurolyte: Enhances our ability to work magic, manifest, and commune with elemental and nature spirits. Provides protection in the astral field and against the dark arts.

Sugilite: Helps to effect deep, transformative healing, growth, and evolution by raising our frequency so that we are more attuned to receiving vibrations of light and pure energy from Source. Helps us to heal on karmic levels from past-life wounding, and supports us in making choices in this lifetime that are more in alignment with our hearts and souls. Beneficial in psychic development, especially if there is fear or karma blocking our psychic abilities.

Thulite: Emits vibrations of divine love, compassion, and sweetness, and stimulates the mother principle in all of us that is part of the divine feminine.

Tiger's eye: Grounding, stabilizing energy that helps to maintain a balanced flow of chi through the solar plexus chakra.

Topaz, clear: Amplifies and accelerates manifestation, particularly when used in conjunction with visualization and meditation.

Topaz, golden or imperial: Increases our inner sense of wealth, worth, and abundance, so that we're more attuned to those frequencies in our outer world, and more likely to both attract and take action toward manifesting prosperity, abundance, and material wealth in our daily lives.

Tourmaline, blue: Stimulates the psychic functions of both the throat and the third eye chakras, particularly enhancing our clairaudient abilities.

Unakite: Begins to undo our illusion of separation between our spiritual selves and experiences, and our physical selves and experiences. In so doing, we are better able to free ourselves from what is expected of us or what we feel we should do with our lives, and brings greater awareness to the longing of our hearts and the guidance of our souls.

Aura-clearing and healing properties of the listed crystals:

Amethyst: Wards away negativity, and the anxiety or fear that can arise from psychic attack and weaken our natural defenses or resolve.

Aragonite star cluster: Emits high-frequency vibrations, similar in quality to that of the Christ Consciousness. Activates healing on all levels and dispels lower, harmful vibrations.

Bloodstone: Fortifies and stabilizes the energy of the physical body, so that more energy can be directed to healing the auric fields.

Blue kyanite: Creates a protective barrier around an aura or chakra and helps to repel dark spirits and vibrations.

Fluorite: Cloaks and shields the aura and chakras from psychic attack, curses, and energy directed at us with malevolent intention.

Healer's gold: Restores the power and balance of the solar plexus chakra while blocking any lower, harmful vibes.

Infinite: Revitalizes and strengthens our auric and etheric fields, which supports the healing and fortification of those fields. Revitalizes and replenishes energy systems with Earth chi.

Labradorite: Creates a protective shield or barrier for the heart chakra, and helps to increase the power of the heart's energy field.

Obsidian, black: I commonly refer to black obsidian as the "witch's stone," because it repels the darkness attracted by our own shadows and shields us from curses, ill-wishes, dark magic, and spirits.

Quartz, aqua aura: Creates an additional layer of etheric protection around our aura.

Quartz, elestial: Dissolves and resolves psychic debris, repels negative spirit or thought-form attachments, and shields the aura.

Quartz, smoky: Helps to clear and release lower, harmful energies, and psychic and spirit attachments.

Quartz, spirit: Raises the frequency of our auric fields, dissolving or repelling psychic debris.

Quartz, tourmaline: The energy-clearing and shielding properties of black tourmaline are amplified and magnified within the quartz, helping to clear and repel lower, harmful frequencies.

Selenite: Rapidly or instantly dissolves lower, harmful, frequencies, especially those that contain density that can lead to energy blockages and accumulation of psychic debris. Raises the frequency of all energy vibrations, exposing them to the divine light spectrum so that they are dissolved and resolved in divine light.

Tourmaline, black: Rapidly intensifies energy vibrations, increasing their frequencies, and repelling any lower, harmful vibrations that cannot match those high frequencies. Excellent for shielding the aura and for overall psychic and energy protection.

GLOSSARY

Akashic records: A realm of light and consciousness where the information of all lives—past, present, and future—is stored.

Amulet: An object that, when worn or carried, is believed to provide protection against all forms of evil, harm, danger, and disease.

Angel: Benevolent, celestial, supernatural, non-gendered being that carries out God's will and serves as a messenger or intermediary between the realms of heaven and Earth.

Ascended masters: Beings who were once human, but, having undergone spiritual initiations and transformations, have become enlightened. They exist in the spirit world and continue to serve as benevolent teachers for humanity.

Astral plane: A plane of existence that is composed of subtle energy, and is inhabited by departed souls and other nonphysical entities and spirits.

Aura: A subtle energy field that is generated by, and surrounds, all living beings.

Biofield: The electromagnetic field that is generated by, and surrounds, all living beings.

Chakra: A Sanskrit word that means "spinning wheel of light." Chakras are major energy centers that overlie major nerve plexuses and organs in the body. Chakras have their own unique colors and frequencies, spin at their own velocities, and are associated with subtle energy fields in the aura.

Charm: An ornament or object, worn by a person, that is considered to have magical power, and can provide protection against harm or attract good fortune.

Chi, or qi: Vital energy that surrounds, penetrates, and animates all life. Also known as prana.

Clairaudience: The power or psychic ability to hear things on the astral plane.

Claircognizance: The psychic ability or power to have, receive, and understand information from subtle realms.

Clairsentience: The psychic ability to feel, sense, or perceive energy.

Clairvoyance: The psychic ability to see or perceive things that are beyond our physical reality.

Crystal: A solid whose atoms are arranged in a regular, ordered, repeating geometric pattern, forming symmetrically arranged plane surfaces.

Divine feminine: A universal frequency of female, cosmic mother, queen, and Goddess consciousness.

Divine masculine: A universal frequency of male, cosmic father, warrior, and God consciousness.

Electromagnetic field: A field, made up of electric and magnetic components, that creates an electric charge, with a definite amount of electromagnetic energy.

Empath: A person highly sensitive to energy who absorbs or is affected by other people's emotions, frequencies, and vibrations, and is influenced by the energy around him or her. A projecting empath influences or affects other people and the energy around them with his or her own feelings.

Entity: In energy healing, an entity is a subtle body, form, or spirit on the astral plane that has an independent existence and level of consciousness.

Etheric bonds: Subtle or psychic ties, cords, or attachments that link us to others. These bonds are neutral in nature and can channel energy, ranging from harmful vibrations to those of light and love.

Frequency: The number of complete oscillations per second of energy in the form of waves.

Geopathic stress: A distorted or disrupted electromagnetic field from the Earth, commonly caused by fault lines, underground waterways, sewage or subway systems, mineral formations, and underground cavities or caverns. Time spent in areas of geopathic stress can lead to poor health and well-being.

Higher realms: Nonphysical planes of existence.

Homeostasis: A state of equilibrium.

Karma: A law that is triggered and a force that is generated by a person's actions, as taught in Hindu and Buddhist belief systems, that has ethical or balancing consequences for a person's next life or existence.

Law of attraction: One of twelve metaphysical laws based on similar lessons or themes taught in various sacred texts and scriptures throughout human history. The law of attraction states that like attracts like. Negative energy will attract more negative energy, and positive energy will attract more positive energy.

Medical qigong: An ancient form of Chinese energy medicine that seeks to correct bioenergetic imbalances and blockages in the body to bring about and maintain good health.

Meridiens: Energy pathways or channels that flow through and access all parts of the body, forming a distribution network of chi.

Nadis: Energy channels or streams that flow through the body and form a distribution network of prana (chi) to all parts and areas of the body.

Parasitic attachment: Attachment to humans by spiritual, psychic, or subtle energy bowdies, typically by means of a psychic cord. Parasitic attachments feed or siphon off that being's chi, or life-force energy. They are distinct formations that can be non-intelligent in nature, but do have their own kind of independent consciousness.

Past lives: Lives lived or experienced before this lifetime through the process of reincarnation, where a soul incarnates multiple times on the Earth plane.

Prana: Vital energy that surrounds, penetrates, and animates all life. Also known as chi or qi.

Psychic cord: In energy healing, this term typically refers to unhealthy psychic bonds or subtle energy connections that form between people, but can also form between people and their thoughts, spirits, or entities, even places. The energy being channeled through these cords is considered harmful or unhealthy, and can also be a conduit through which malevolent spirits or entities siphon or feed off a being's chi or life force.

Receptive side or hand: Receptive refers to the non-dominant hand or non-dominant side of the body, which receives or allows energy to enter the system, as opposed to the dominant or active hand or side that casts or propels energy out of the system.

Spirit guides: Divinely appointed, nonphysical beings that are always present with you and are assigned to help protect, guide, and support you.

Subtle body: A field of energy that connects to or surrounds the body, or that exists as its own formation on the astral plane. While it is not veritable it can be perceived by the psychic senses.

Subtle channels: Channels of energy that are not veritable but that can be perceived by the psychic senses.

Subtle energy: Energy that cannot be measured by current scientific methods, but that can be perceived by the psychic senses.

Subtle fields: See subtle body.

Talisman: An object that, when worn or carried, is believed to attract love or good fortune.

Thought-form: A structured energy formation that is created by focused mental energy, and can be psychically programmed to carry out a specific task (e.g., delivering a curse).

Traditional Chinese medicine (TCM): Medical practices based on thousands of years of Chinese tradition, including the use of mind-body practices like qigong, massage, and acupuncture, as well as herbal and dietary remedies to treat or prevent health problems.

Transference: The act or process of energy being transferred between one object or being and another.

Transmutation: In energy healing, when negative energy is transformed into positive energy or light, it is referred to as transmutation. It is the conversion of one level or form of energy into another.

Veritable: Able to be measured by current scientific methods.

Vibration: The oscillation of an electromagnetic wave, or of a particle of matter whose equilibrium has been disturbed.

BIBLIOGRAPHY AND RESOURCES

Bibliography

Dale, Cyndi. *The Subtle Body: An Encyclopedia of Your Energetic Anatomy.* Boulder, CO: Sounds True, Inc., 2009.

Judith, Anodea. *Wheels of Life: A User's Guide to the Chakra System.* Woodbury, MN: Llewellyn Publications, 1999.

Kunz, George Frederick. *The Curious Lore of Precious Stones.* New York: Dover Publications, Inc., 1971.

Rand, William L. Reiki: *The Healing Touch First and Second Degree Manual.* Southfield, MI: The Center for Reiki Training, 1996.

Resources

Readers who would like to learn more about Krista Mitchell's professional crystal healer and reader certifications, crystal workshops, special events, and trainings are encouraged to visit her website: **krista-mitchell.com.**

For photos of crystals and to learn more about their metaphysical properties, Krista recommends the following books:

Hall, Judy. *The Crystal Bible.* London, UK: Godsfield Press, 2003.

Melody. *Love is in the Earth: A Kaleidoscope of Crystals.* Wheat Ridge, CO: Earth-Love Publishing House, 2002.

Simmons, Robert, and Naisha Ahsian. *The Book of Stones: Who They Are and What They Teach.* East Montpelier, VT: Heaven & Earth Publishing, LLC., Berkeley, CA: North Atlantic Books, 2005.

To learn more about the shadow and shadow-self healing, Krista recommends reading the following works of Debbie Ford:

Ford, Debbie. *The Dark Side of the Light Chasers.* New York, NY: Riverhead Books, 2010.

Ford, Debbie. *The Secret of the Shadow: The Power of Owning Your Whole Story.* New York, NY: HarperCollins Publishers Inc., 2002.

ACKNOWLEDGMENTS

First and foremost, I thank my clients for trusting me with their healing process, for their courage and grace, and for allowing me to be part of their journey to wellness.

I thank my crystals. To this day, they are still my greatest healers, teachers, and guides. I am beyond blessed that I found you (or that you found me).

I thank Kate Zimmermann for her belief in this book, and everyone at Sterling Publishing for blessing me with the opportunity of bringing this book out into the world.

My sincerest, heartfelt gratitude to my friend Nicholas Pepe, who blessed this book with his magic, and who gave me wise, honest, and constructive feedback throughout.

I thank Susan Lander for her mentorship, wisdom, and kindness. Ingrid Aybar for being a warrior of light, and reminding me that my story deserves to be told. Elsa Mehary for her insight, honesty, and steadfast support.

I thank my dear sweet mum, who loves me just the way I am, reminds me to stay strong, and was willing to give crystal healing a shot (and now loves it!). And my two wee doggies, Gaby and Muppet, who are truly my greatest teachers in presence, compassion, patience, and unconditional love.

And last, but not least, I thank the healers and teachers who supported me on my own path and who had an indelible impact on my work: Anjelika Kremer, Michel Chevalier, Margaret Ann Case, Jodi St. Onge, Debbie Ford and the Ford Institute, Catherine Greene, and Colleen Duffy.

INDEX